# PRACTICAL APPROACH TO EDUCATIONAL TECHNOLOGY

# Practical Approach to
# Educational Technology

*Edited by*
**Dr. Vachan Singh**
M.Sc., B.Ed., Ph.D.

**AKANSHA PUBLISHING HOUSE**
**NEW DELHI - 110 059 (INDIA)**

**AKANSHA PUBLISHING HOUSE**
R-37-B, Vani Vihar
Uttam Nagar
New Delhi - 110 059

*Showroom*
4679/21-B, Ansari Road
Daryaganj, New Delhi - 110 002
Phones: 9811582579, 9212065579

*Practical Approach to Educational Technology*

First Published, 2005
Reprint–2006
Reprinted : 2010

PRINTED IN INDIA

Published by M.P. Misra for Akansha Publishing House, New Delhi - 110 059 and Printed at Tarun Offset Press, Delhi.

*Dedicated*

*to*

*Great Pioneers in the Field of Education*

# Contents

# Preface

> "Educational Technology is concerned with the application of modern skills and techniques to education."
>
> —Derik Unwin

In a technical sense, education refers to that process by which society, through its different institutions, deliberately transmits its cultural heritage to its young—its accumulated values, knowledge and skills—from one generation to another.

Education is an acquired experience of any sort—intellectual, emotional or sensory-motor. Education is a product of experience. It proceeds from birth to death and the agencies that impart education are the school, home, press, radio, television, religion, cinema and other modes of mass media etc. But life involves constant and continuous modification of experience because attitudes, opinions etc. constantly undergo alterations, and education is that process which helps the child to adjust to this changing world. It is here that technology comes to our help in modernizing the society.

Educational technology can be considered as the systematic use of scientific methods to plan, realise and evaluate effective teaching and learning process in informal and non-informal situations. Educational technology as it exists today is comparatively a new idea; grown as a result of the integration of technological devices in the use of practices with the newly explored psychological principles of learning, teaching, behavioural modification, content analysis, education etc. The term connotes a field of study including instructional design, audiovisual media, learning process, teaching strategies and evaluation techniques. Educational technology has come to stay as a discipline with a number of interrelated concepts and applications. Since the develcpment of radio, people have proposed that communications technology provide major improvements in the delivery of education.

In the present age of advanced information technology, knowledge dissemination has become highly technology-oriented. Difficult subject-matter can be made easily understood. Complicated matters and structures, as in case of Biology, can be taught precisely with the help of visual aids.

Amidst the plenty of literature, here we have attempted to present the succinct information on Basic elements of educational technology; educational technology; scope and meaning of ET; nature and scope of ET; transfer of training; frontiers of ET; learning and ET; Environmentalism as teaching technique; teaching technology: discovery and diffusion etc.

Usually, books of such complex nature are developed on empirical knowledge put forward by different experts in the field. Often the facts are told and retold. We do not claim any originality. The great pioneers in the field of education who have propounded various theories after painstaking research deserve appreciation.

The entire information herein is gathered from secondary sources—books, abstracts, journals, magazines and proceedings etc. Thus, we have tried to compile the relevant material in a sequence for the benefit of readers. The credit goes to different scholars and academics of eminence in the field whose views, exercises and works are liberally cited and substantially borrowed. I owe a deep sense of gratitude to them all. Wherever possible, we have acknowledged and whose names could not be traced, I acknowledge a profound sense of gratefulness to them all.

I am thankful to my friends, colleagues, senior teachers

and my family members for their constant inspiration and moral support. I cannot forget my wife, son and daughter who provided a congenial atmosphere at home for work. Last but not the least, I am thankful to my publisher for materialising my present endeavour.

**—VS**

# 1

# Basic Elements of Educational Technology

The term Educational Technology connotes a field of study including instructional design, audiovisual media, learning process, teaching strategies and evaluation techniques. Although there is a growing agreement that educational technology should include the subjects of educational psychology, principles of communication, educational management, etc., some educationists continue to ascribe a low profile of mere educational resources to it. Nevertheless, educational technology has come to stay as a discipline with a number of interrelated concepts and applications. It is only appropriate to begin by looking at the basic concept as also the general framework of educational technology.

What can be the prerequisite or a precondition for those willing to peep into the field of educational technology? Just an open mind will do. In fact, it is more like an invitation to all interested to the reception hosted in honour of the new words Education and Technology! The couple constitutes an exciting subject to us who have chosen to be in the domain of education.

### Modular Objectives

On studying this module, you will be able to: define the

term 'educational technology; outline the scope of educational technology; describe a number of related concepts; and, Differentiate between educational technology and audiovisual aids.

Attempt the following questions and determine whether you are already aware of the basic definitions and concepts in educational technology. If you score over 80%, you may skip the module; if not, it is worth going through it!

**What is Educational Technology?**

Technology refers to the techniques. A systematic way of applying the techniques to achieve an objective is as important as the use of technical equipment for the same. As a matter of fact, techniques are reckoned as the software and the equipment as the hardware of technology. Technology results in new designs and devices as also new ideas and processes. Each new physical device is accompanied by a new set of procedures and techniques. For example, the development of telephone has led to phone books, answering machines, Fax, telephone shopping etc. The 'hard' component (physical device) may be differentiated- from the 'soft' component (methodologies) for the purpose of study.

Education the act or process of acquiring and imparting knowledge, is crucial to the development of a learner with a view to his/her participation in the transformation of the world for a better tomorrow. Learning and understanding are basic to the definition of education.

Educational technology is not a simple combination of these two words . It is usually thought of even more than the sum of the following-two interpretations:

(a) Technology in education

(b) Technology of education

| | Questions for Self-Assessment | Points Allocated | Your Score |
|---|---|---|---|
| 1. | State one standard definition of educational technology: | 3 | |
| 2. | Technology in education refers to the .............concept and technology of education implies the ............. orientation of educational technology | 2 | |
| 3. | Mention two factors in the instructional design process: | 2 | |
| 4. | Classify the following as hardware or software:<br>(a) Reference books<br>(b) Blank cassettes<br>(c) Chalkboard<br>(d) Computer animation<br>(e) Video programmes | 5 | |
| 5. | Mention two components of the educational technology system: | 2 | |
| 6. | What should a learning resource centre have?<br>Software: .............<br>Hardware: ............. | 4 | |
| 7. | State two methods of improving teaching-learning effectiveness | 2 | |
| | | Total : | 20 |
| | | Your % Score : | |

Early developments referred to fee role of technology in education which signify the use of audiovisual equipment, e.g., hardware in educational processes. Later developments recognise the concept of technology of education, i.e., techniques and methodologies of the teaching-learning process. This is indeed the software aspect of educational technology. The origin of software is closely associated with the course ware, i.e., instructional design and development of a subject.

Use of technology in training results in increased productivity through enhanced human capability. Use of technology in education results in increased effectiveness of the educational process. For example, telephone extends our capability to talk and listen over long distance and automobile extends our capability to travel large distance over short period of time. Overhead projectors extend our capabilities to project a large image of a visual on a screen and slides enable us to capture real-life events and bring them into the classroom.

Audiovisuals have been on the move, for quite sometime now. They have made an impact in many different situations, e.g., seminars, conferences, extension lectures, meetings, research and project report presentations. Classrooms are also beginning to feel their influence!

"Educational Technology is a systematic way of designing, implementing and evaluating the total process of learning and teaching in terms of specific objectives, based on research in human learning and communication and employing a combination of human and non-human resources to bring about more effective instruction." [Commission on Instructional Technology, US].

"Educational Technology is a complex, integrated process involving people, procedures, ideas, devices, and organization, for analyzing problems and devising, implementing, evaluating, and managing solutions to those problems, involved in all aspects of learning." [Association for Educational Communications and Technology, USA].

"Educational Technology is the development, application and evaluation of systems, techniques and aids to improve the process of human learning." [Council for Educational Technology, UK].

"Educational Technology is the application of scientific knowledge about learning, and the conditions of learning, to improve the effectiveness and efficiency of teaching and training. In the absence of scientifically established principles, educational technology implements techniques of empirical testing to improve learning situations." [National Centre for Programmed Learning, UK].

A close look at the definitions reveals that they underline educational technology as a systematic way, a process or an application of the scientific knowledge, to improve the efficiency of the process of learning and instruction. It is thus considered to be the technology of education more than the technology in education.

## Educational Technology: Development and Growth

The subject of educational technology has developed over three aspects after the World War-II:

> *Mass Communication, Individual Learning, and Group Learning Strategies.*
>
> According to Elton, each of these aspects has passed through the following three phases:
>
> Research (R), Development (D) and Use (U)

## Educational Technology vs Audiovisual Aids

Educational technology is a vast subject concerned with the application of scientific knowledge about learning and conditions of learning in order to improve the effectiveness of teaching, learning and evaluation. Audiovisuals are merely the aids or resources, i.e., materials which are employed to improve the quality of the message. Audio-visuals are a part of a subject of Educational Technology.

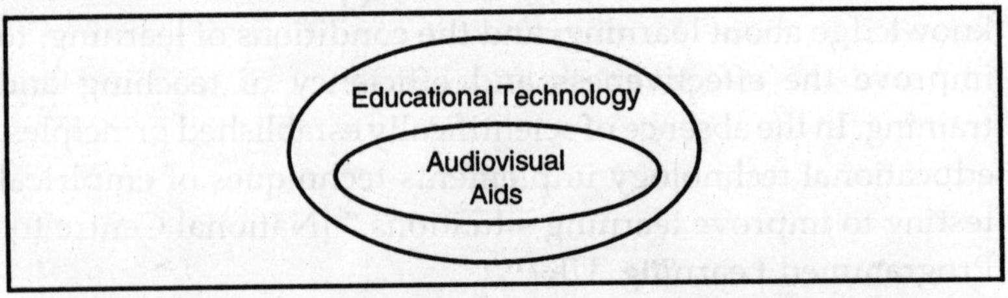


**Fig. 1.** Audiovisual Aids as Educational Technology Subset.

## EDUCATIONAL TECHNOLOGY *VS.* AUDIOVISUAL AIDS

| *Audiovisual Aids* | *Educational Technology* |
|---|---|
| Audiovisuals are material products which may be used or misused. design. | Educational technology connotes processes and products of instructional |
| Audiovisual aids are physical objects. | Educational technology is a vast subject. |
| Audiovisuals consist of print matter projected and electronics resources such as slides, video and computers. | The subject of educational technology encompasses learning psychology, communication and advances in science and technology. |
| Audiovisuals improve the quality of the message; they impart audio and visual dimensions to it. | Educational technology aims at improving all aspects of communication, i.e., encoding, message, channel, barriers, decoding retention and application. |
| Audiovisual aids exist without regard to group dynamics and individual differences. | Educational technology deals with the processes of implementing methods and resources with regard to group dynamics and individual differences. |
| Audiovisual aids are different for different topics and subjects. They fit in a currriculum. | Educational technology principles are applicable to all topics and subjects and hence basic to all curriculum development. |
| Audiovisuals are products of technology alone. They are technical gadgets. | Educational technology is a great deal more than technology; it is based on psychology, social anthropology, etc. |
| Audiovisuals stand alone. These are unrelated articles. | Educational technology is a system with a number of interconnected and interdependent components. |

Mass instruction or mass communication was the first one to be taken up around 1940. Research and development led to the use of radio, television broadcast and closed circuit television (CCTV) for mass instruction. More people could be educated faster and better without multiplying the number of teachers, classrooms and associated resources. Closed circuit television systems were installed for large classes and for subjects which were taught repetitively. The practice was not favoured by many as it lacked feedback and interactivity. Most programmes were roughly produced, presented and applied. The practice was, therefore, discontinued. But radio and television broadcast techniques survived some how.

Skinner proposed that learning takes place through a cycle of stimulus, response and reinforcement. It resulted in linear programming and later, in branched programme learning. Individualised learning became the focus of many researches in the fifties. Coupled, with Skinner's behavioural psychology, it led to the development of individualised learning packages. Attempts to design programmed instruction texts and teaching machines signaled the inadequacy of the simplistic models of learning. A revival of individualised learning has taken place with the use of computers in education.

On the contrary, the group learning aspect of educational technology began to be favoured in view of its potential to develop group skills such as discussion and interpersonal skills. Research on group learning came about with the humanistic psychology due to Rogers. The technique of group dynamics refers to the interactive process of learning from one another in small group situations. Simulation, role-play, games and case studies are some of the group learning techniques. The hardware and software required for group learning are only those which help in simulation, presentation of case studies, games, etc.

## Technology and Instructional Design

By instructional design we mean the strategic design and

development of instruction for the desired objectives. It incorporates the theories of learning, principles of communication and hypotheses for interest, motivation and participation of learners. Instructional technology implies the techniques and methodologies of instruction, i.e., technology of instruction. It does not place any emphasis on audiovisual aids *per se*. Therefore, instructional design and technology are, linked with the effectiveness and efficiency of the teaching-learning process.

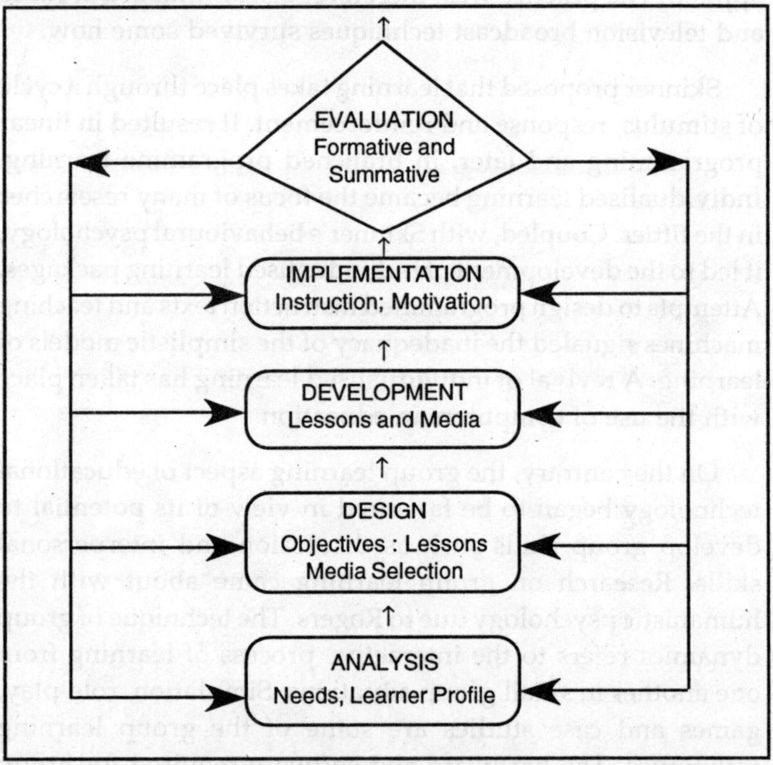


**Fig. 2.** Development of Instructional Systems.

The above schematic diagram shows that an instructional system is developed by analysing the needs of learners, designing the curriculum, developing the lessons and media, implementation of instruction and finally evaluating the progress and also terminal abilities of the students.

## Media and Audiovisual Resources

An aural message is perhaps the minimum required for communication. It is often necessary to supplement the aural message with a visual in order to convey it effectively. Visuals with or without aural components are called audiovisual resources, aids, media or simply audiovisuals. Audiovisuals resources consist of hardware and software components. In fact, for every hardware, there is a corresponding software.

**EDUCATIONAL HARDWARE AND CORRESPONDING SOFTWARE**

| Hardware | Software |
|---|---|
| Overhead projector | Overhead transparencies |
| Blank paper | Written matter |
| Slide projector | Slides |
| Computer | Computer programme |
| Audio-recorder | Recorded audio |
| VCR and Monitor | Video programme |
| Chalkboard | Chalkwork |

The audio component may be added to any one of the above resources. It may either be with recorded voice on cassettes, tapes and discs or it may be lived oral message by the presenter. Sometimes, the audio through a recorder or radio broadcast may be the only channel for the message.

In view of the wide range of audiovisuals, hey are best classified as non-projected, projected and electronic resources as shown in Fig. 3.

Audiovisual software is prepared through the steps of preparing instructional design, development and associated processes, e.g., writing, printing and recording. Even so, some early developments denounced all audiovisuals as technology in education and thus narrowed down the scope of educational technology to the mechanical use of audiovisual components. This view is no longer tenable since the basis of audiovisual education goes deep into the psychology of learning and effective communication.

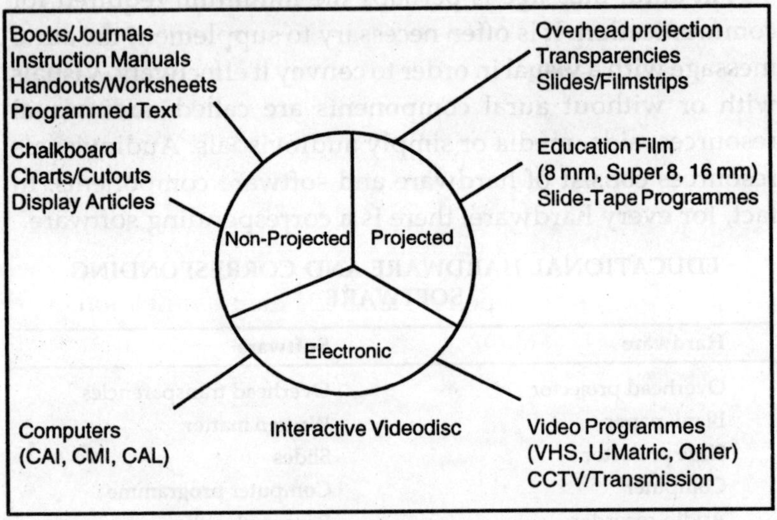


**Fig. 3.** Classification of Audiovisuals

Mass media may, however, overlap with audiovisuals for communication. Use of radio, telephone and television in broadcast, cable or closed-circuit modes may well be educationally meaningful if the message is identified through instructional design and development processes. Techniques such as previewing the programme, preparing the audience to look for the intended information in advance of the programme and following up the sessions with further questions and discussions, etc. are very useful activities. Furthermore, it is the effective use of the audio or video programme that makes it educationally powerful.

## System of Education Technology

A 'system' is an assemblage of interconnected and interacting components. All the components which comprise the system are conceptualised to be bounded by an imaginary boundary for the purpose of identifying the system. The 'region' outside the system boundary represents the conditions under which the system operates; it is referred to as the environment for the system.

One may choose to include any number and size of components to constitute a system for a desired purpose. For example, the entire universe with all the creations of God, Man and the Devil may be considered as a system; a biological cell, a television, a TV tube, an institute, an industry are some further examples of systems. A system may consist of subsystems, which when combined constitute the system.

Closed systems and open systems are the classification of systems. When a system operates in isolation from the environment, i.e., without any effect or transaction from the environment it is said to be a dosed system. On the other hand if a system interacts with the environment by way of some input and output, it is called an open system. The input may consist of raw material information, energy or human beings and the output may be finished products or qualified persons. The purpose of an open system may be to convert the given input into the desired output. An industry, an institute, and a car engine are examples of open systems. In that case, the system is indeed a transformation function, which is either a process or a series of processes.

Educational technology may be viewed as a system in terms of systems approach, with a number of subsystems and components or elements.

Tackling the interacting subsystems or components of the educational technology system is referred to as the systems approach in dealing with institutional problems and developmental issues. It brings into focus the process and the product orientation of educational technology.

The process concept directs our attention to the components of needs assessment, goal analysis, task analysis, curriculum design, selection of instructional delivery systems, production and utilisation of media as also the formative and summative evaluation. The product orientation of educational technology makes reference to the audiovisual devices and hardware. The total system consists of interacting processes and products employed fat the desired educational goals. It is desirable to learn in detail about the subsystems and components of educational technology system before taking up optimisation of the whole system. The systems approach helps us to identify the effectiveness and the weak points of subsystems and hence the means through which instructional systems can operate at optimum efficiencies.

**Characteristics of Systems**

1. A system is a relative concept; it can be a subsystem of a larger system!
2. All systems are directed to achieve certain goals and outputs under some constraints and with given inputs.
3. A system may be dosed or open-ended.
4. All systems may be optimised by way of considering the variables alternatives, feedback processes, etc.
5. A system refers to a collective entity consisting of a group of inter-related and interacting elements.

Inputs to the system are the entry-profile of the student, audiovisual and other resources; the system results in improved exit-profile of students. It also shows the interaction of elements and the iterative nature of the teaching-learning-evaluation process. The starting point is the learning objectives from which content is derived.

A teaching-learning strategy is identified as also appropriate audiovisual material and other resources are taken in. Learning thus created in students is evaluated. If the learning is short of the objective, the strategy and learning process are reviewed. If the objective is achieved, the next objective is taken up and so on. It may be observed that the objectives play a multiple role in the total process. Content, i.e, subject matter is determined from the objectives; teaching methods and audiovisual resources are identified in view of the intended objectives and finally, the learning outcome of students is measured against the same terminal objectives.

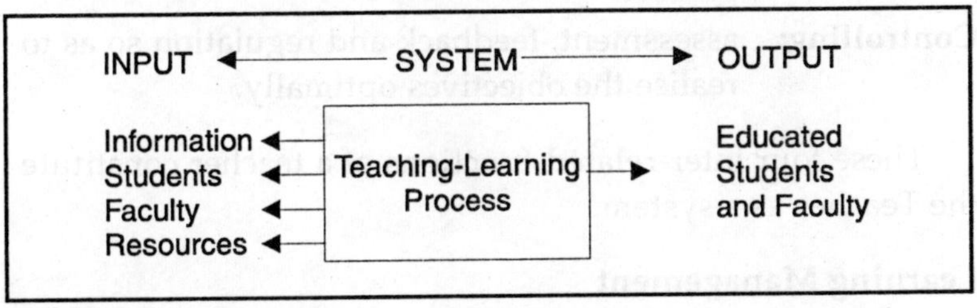


**Fig. 4.** Systems Model of the Teaching-Learning Process?

System concept of educational technology permits us to optimise the effetiveness of whatever it is applied to Educational technology improves the teaching-learning process in a classroom by way of the following:

1. by decreasing student frustration and by increasing teacher satisfaction. Effectiveness of an educational process is not improved merely by the introduction of technology into it. It is, in fact, a function of human skills of employing the technology as also the hardware and software components of technology.
2. by reducing the time for learning the same thing and increasing the learning outcome over the same time,
3. by lowering the percentage dropout and increasing student achievement,

## Role of Teachers

The role of a teacher is characterised by the following four broad functions:

**Planning:** establishment of the objectives, preparation of units and schedule of training, etc.

**Organising:** arrangement of the learning resources, distillation of audiovisuals, etc.

**Leading:** motivation, encouragement and provision of stimuli to the students in the teaching-learning process.

**Controlling:** assessment, feedback and regulation so as to realise the objectives optimally.

These four inter-related functions of a teacher constitute the Teacher as a system.

## Learning Management

With the ever-increasing availability of audiovisual resources and greater knowledge of the learning process, the primary role of a teacher is to be a Resource Person and manager of resources.

Libraries of books and journals are being converted into Learning Resource Centres where a complete range of software is available. Videocasettes, slide series, tape-slide programmes, computer software and overhead transparencies are being added and cross-referred to learning resource centres. With greater emphasis on the development of resources with the participation of teachers likely to use these resources, Resource Centres are being set up where groups of teachers take up joint projects of audiovisual resource development. Likewise, they take up the production of modules on different topics.

Modular format of instruction has created new interest form the point of view of self-instruciton and individualised instruction. A learning resource centre may well be equipped with a number of viewing cabins for video viewing and work-tables for interactive use of computer software. VCRs, monitors and headphones are installed for the former and computer terminals or personal computers for the latter.

More and more libraries are being networked for providing access to books and journals as also bibliographies of research on different topics. This is made possible through computer and video technologies.

Research had proved that learning is individual to a learner. The teacher-centered approach of teaching is, therefore, being transformed into learner-centered methods of learning.

Courses on Study Skills and Techniques of Learning may be given to students early in their adolescence so that they should take over the responsibility of learning and employ efficient methods of learning in classrooms, reading books and using other software as also from the world of work. Teaching students to learn for themselves and enabling them to learn how to study effectively is perhaps the latest development in educational technology.

## Useful Guidelines

### *Library Assignment to Locate References*

- Visit your library and note down the Titles/Authors/Acc. Nos. of the books in the area of Educational Technology.
- Also note down the titles of the journals in the area of Educational Technology, Audiovisuals, Education Television, Computers, Instruction, etc.
- Scan through at least one of the references and state what you feel about it.

## *Post-Module Self-Assessment*

Attempt the following questions and determine whether you have achieved the objectives of the module. A score of 80% or more spells success!

| Questions for Self-Assessment | Points Allocated | Your Score |
|---|---|---|
| 1. State one standard definition of educational technology:<br>........................................<br>........................................ | 3 | |
| 2. Technology in education refers to the ................concept and technology of education implies the ............... orientation of educational technology | 2 | |
| 3. Mention two factors in the instructional design process:<br>........................................<br>........................................ | 2 | |
| 4. Classify the following as hardware or software:<br>(a) Reference books<br>(b) Blank cassettes<br>(c) Chalkboard<br>(d) Computer animation<br>(e) Video programmes | 5 | |
| 5. Mention tow components of the educational technology system: | 2 | |
| 6. What should a learning resources centre have?<br>Software: ............................<br>Hardware: ........................... | 4 | |
| 7. State two methods of improving teaching-learning effectiveness<br>................................................... | 2 | |
| Total : | 20 | |
| Your % Score : | | |

## Summing Up

It is evident from the foregoing discussion that Educational technology implies more than the sum total of all the media, methods, materials and techniques used for better teaching and learning. Educational technology has enabled us to integrate the process of instructional design and the development of instructional media. Advances in educational sciences on the one hand and in optical and electronic technologies on the other have provided an excellent scenario for a new range of developments in order to make the teaching-learning-evaluation process more efficient and accessible.

## ANSWERS TO SELF-ASSESSMENT QUESTIONS

1. One of the four definitions from the text.
2. Product; process.
3. Theories of learning; principles of communication.
4. Software, hardware, hardware, software, software.
5. Audiovisual resources, teaching methods, evaluation.
6. Books, journals, audiovisual and computer software; VCRs and PCs.
7. Formulating objectives, employing audiovisuals, teaching study skills, etc.

## QUESTIONS

1. Why is educational technology referred to as a system? What are its subsystems? Give examples of some systems models in educational technology.
2. Educational technology is widely accepted as the sum of technology in education and technology of education. Explain this concept and relate it to the hardware plus software concept of educational technology.
3 Explain the concept and scope of educational technology. Draw up a comparison between educational technology and audiovisual resources.

4 Discuss the promise educational technology holds for us in terms of media and methods in the formal and informal modes of teaching and learning.

5. How does the system concept of educational technology help in optimising the effectiveness of an educational process? Does it contribute to the management of learning, planning for teaching and instructional design? Explain.

# 2

# Educational Technology

It has not been possible in India so far to develop a theoretical model to define the concept and practices in the field of educational technology. Efforts have been made at the All India level to publish some material in the form of the year book of educational technology and bring out a journal by the association of educational technology. But they are mainly a conglomeration of stray thoughts by individuals and have no connection to research or experimentation in the field of educational technology. The concepts have only been borrowed and have been prevented without clear perception on the subject.

The fact however, remains that in a country like India where 64 per cent people are illiterate, newer methods of teaching are needed to convey the messages easily and rapidly to the educators. Local research is needed in the field. So far only American concepts are being blindly followed by the Indian education Pundits both in the bureaucracy and in the schools/colleges and other institutions.

## Impact of Information Technology on Education

Since the development of the radio, people have proposed that communications technology provide major improvements in the delivery of education. Research on "teaching machines" dates back to the 1940's, before the general introduction of computers into the marketplace. Since that time, there has been continual research, development, and implementation of techniques for using information technology in various aspects of education.

OTA investigated what is known and what has been proposed about possible applications of information technology to education. Information technology is capable of becoming a major resource for the delivery of educational services over the coming decade:

- — IT can be an effective delivery mechanism for most existing forms of education.
- — IT provides capabilities for responding to new demands that traditional schoolroom education cannot meet adequately.
- — The cost of information products and services for educational applications will continue to drop with respect to other items in the educational budget.

The main advantages will be realised from combinations of new technologies rather than from any single device. Most educational applications will be based on hardware technology that is originally developed for a broader consumer market. The only exceptions will be devices designed for specialised industrial uses—e.g., flight training for airline pilots—or education and training for the handicapped.

It is not possible to predict with certainty the technological base that will exist for educational use. Some of the products and services now projected for the next decade, may not survive the competition, for the consumer's money. This uncertainty may inhibit the rapid development of software and services particularly education market-oriented.

The provision of high-quality, reasonably priced educational software is the principal technological challenge.

Low-cost hardware will be widely available to most homes, offices, and schools.

## Functions of Educational Technology

Computers and communications technology can provide educational services in many ways. In some cases, different types of applications will require different technologies; in other cases, the same type of technology can be used to provide different types of services.

### *Passive Instruction*

The oldest instructional use of information technology is simply to present information. The textbook is the traditional passive instructional system. Projection media—slides, filmstrips, overhead transparencies, and pictures—are more modern forms. Educational radio and television have experienced quiet but steady growth since the late 1950's and early 1960's. Video cassettes and video disks will provide even more flexible tools for presenting video-based instructional material.

The best known recent examples of passive instructional programming are the "Sesame Street" and "Electric Company" programmes produced by the Children's Television Workshop with partial Federal support. These programmes were intended to supplement, not replace, normal schooling. Sesame Street is intended to teach preschool children some 'basic concepts and learning' attitudes. Electric Company is principally aimed at supplementing reading, instruction at the grammar school level. At the other extreme, a full alternative to traditional education is the "Open University" in Britain, which has conducted a full college degree programme for over 11 years, based principally on passive instruction using the broadcast networks.

In the United States, the Corporation for Public Broadcasting is developing an educational programme along similar lines in cooperation with universities across the country. New technology for video production is also having an impact on educational uses. Computer animation systems have become considerably less expensive than older, hand animation techniques. Video processing uses computers to perform elaborate modification of video images. Both of these technologies are widely used in commercial television and motion pictures, but they are, also particularly attractive-for instructional application in which concepts and processes that are subtle and difficult to visualise need to be illustrated.

Complex physical processes; such as fluid flow or load stresses on structures such as bridges, can be simulated on a computer and displayed as dynamic graphic images. In addition, video cassette recorders (VCRs) and video disks promise to relieve students from the dictates of schedule. The VCR, in particular, allows—copyright law permitting—instructors, and students to copy instructional programmes off the air and play them back at - some later time. Video cassettes and video-disks will provide alternate mode of broadcasting for the distribution of instructional material.

**Characteristics of Passive Instruction System**

1. All educational decisions are in the hands of the providers; what information is to be presented, for how long, in what sequence, and even—in the case of such current instructional broadcasting—the schedule—when it is shown.
2. The boundaries between entertainment, public information, and educational services can become blurred. A G.B. Shaw play, a concert, or an informational series such as the successful Cosmos series carried by the Public Broadcasting System, may all the considered important instructional resources as well as entertainment.

### *Interactive Instruction*

Interactive instructional systems require the student to communicate with the device, allowing the system to vary the pace of instruction, select among alternate sequences of presentation, test for understanding, and alter the content according to the specific needs of the individual. This technology is used to teach a specific subject or skill directly to a student, guiding the learner through a sequence of steps involving the presentation of information, drills and exercises designed by an instructor.

Computer-assisted instruction is the best known interactive technology. A student sitting at a computer terminal works through a series of "frames" that teach and test understanding. If the student is progressing slowly, the computer branches to an alternate style of presentation or a remedial section. If the student has mastered that section the computer jumps ahead to more advanced material.

The Plato system was one of the better known experiments. It was developed by researchers at the University of Illinois and Control Data Crop. With principal funding from the Federal Government, the system originally combined a new type of interactive graphics terminal with a large multiterminal computer system and an elaborate language specifically designed to create instructional programmes. While Plato was originally a very expensive experimental system, most of its underlying concepts survive in commercial instructional systems now marketed by Control Data.

Four factors have more recently revived interest in interactive instruction:

(a) the rapidly declining costs of computers and the advent of the desktop computer,

(b) the escalating labour-intensive costs of traditional schooling,

(c) an improved understanding of how to create instructional packages, and

(d) the development of alternative delivery mechanisms —that link the computer with other technologies, such as video disk and interactive cable.

The video disk is good example of how new technologies can be combined to form instructional systems. The video disk contains an extensive data base of text, still images, and film. The computer controls the sequence of presentation and, using an educational programme contained on its floppy disk and information stored in the remote data base, interacts with the student. The video disk, for example, might contain several thousand images of microscope slides. The data base would have full descriptive information on the subjects illustrated by the slides, indexed in various ways.

Educational software on the computer would take a student through sequences of slides and text presentation, providing information and administering tests. While the computer programme would be designed to achieve a specific instructional purpose, the slide catalog and data base would be intended to be more widely applicable for research and education.

Several experiments are being conducted to develop instructional packages, using combinations of video disks and personal computers. The Minnesota Educational Computing Consortium is developing a series of video disks in basic economics. The first disk of a planned 6-disk series has been produced and tried in the classroom with favourable results. Other companies are developing products aimed at the industrial training market; and a few firms, such as IBM, are already using interactive video disks for employee training.

*Characteristics of Interactive Instructional Technology*

1. Because individualisation and self-pacing may not fit well with traditional schooling, large-scale

implementation of interactive instructional technology in the schools may engender substantial institutional resistance.

2 The system can be designed so that students can pace themselves.

3. It allows the system to customise teaching to the particular level of understanding, learning style, and ability of each individual student.

4 The skills required both to produce software and to assist students with its use are substantially different from traditional teaching skills.

5 Smaller instructional modules can be designed to fit into the regular course of instruction, permitting a gradual introduction of educational technology. Principal educational benefits of technology are lost with such an incremental approach.

6 Because they are so carefully tailored, interactive curricular packages are inflexible. They are not generally useful for any purpose, clientele, or environment other than the specific one for which they were designed.

7 Extensive design effort is needed to create each module. The material to be taught must be broken down into framesised pieces. Tests of understanding must be devised, and the paths that students are most likely to take in going through the material must be anticipated.

8 Instructional software is often divided into discrete packages, each designed to teach a specific skill or item of information. An instructional curriculum (say, a fifth grade mathematics course) is a collection of these packages, which, for a full course, may number into the hundreds.

## Learning Environments

As described above, the interactive instruction technology can be used to create a special environment—a language, simulation, or data base—that can be manipulated by the student. For example, special computer languages, such as LOGO, can help learners gain particular problem-solving skills. Languages such as VISICALC, a system designed for business users of small computers, can be a powerful tool in teaching accounting principles and financial planning techniques.

Simulation is the another form of learning environment. A simulation of a laboratory experiment for a physics course, for instance, might present on a television screen a variety of weights and springs. The student would be allowed to connect them in various configurations, to apply forces of prescribed amounts at different points in the arrangement, and to measure and record the results. Working with this system for only a few days, a student would learn some basic principles of mechanics. As another example, large-scale simulations can be made of physical processes or of equipment that might be too expansive or dangerous to use in person. Simulated nuclear power plants provide vehicles for training new operators; simulated aircraft are used for pilot training. For medical education, computer-controlled robots can be used to simulate injured or ill human beings. A small computer presents the student with an instructional sequence where proper techniques are illustrated using a computer-controlled video disk. The student then practices on a dummy equipped with sensors monitored by the computer, which in turn, presents the results.

Simulations of economic and social systems are used to teach political science, economics, and management. Business management games are one of the earliest educational applications of computers, and they have been deeply integrated into the curricula of many business schools. Other educational applications range from simple economic simulations on small computers to elaborate simulations of city management and international politics that require very large computer systems. The Defence Department makes extensive use of computer-based simulations to train senior decision makers in crisis management.

Use and application of information technology to provide a learning environment has several implications:

1. Since the interaction is so flexible and is directed in large part by the students, instructors and student need documentation and supplemental curriculum materials appropriate for using the system to meet their particular educational objectives. Except for large simulations that may require special hardware, the principal cost of "learning environment" applications will be in developing these supplemental curricular materials. Developmental costs for the programmes will, in general, be written off against a much larger customer base.
2. An instructional programme can be applicable over longer course periods and for a greater variety of educational uses than can an interactive module that concentrates on a single teaching unit.
3. Because it fundamentally changes both content and the way material is presented, use of an automated learning environment may require extensive changes in course content or even a broader redesign of an entire curriculum.

**Information Resource**

General information literacy is needed for all individuals to work and to participate fully in an information society. In addition, for most professions, specialised computer and communication-based systems are rapidly becoming indispensable tools of the trade. Students must learn how to use these services as part of their early training.

In addition to being an instructional tool, the computer in education is viewed as an intellectual and problem-solving resource, akin to the library or laboratory, information services will need to be both broad enough to support general education and specialised enough for particular subject matter. Examples of specialised systems include computer-aided design systems for industrial engineering students, on-line legal or medical information retrieval systems for use by law students or doctors, and automated accounting and financial analysis systems.

Besides these specialised resources, students in all fields will need constant access to information services and computer facilities for their work. One engineering school is experimenting with providing a desktop computer to some of its entering freshmen, with a view toward giving computers to all students in the future. A graduate school of business has already adopted a similar policy for its entering students.

The role of the computer as an educational resource on campus is blending with the view of libraries as automated information centres. Many college and university libraries have been among the leaders in this movement—first in automating their management, then in providing users access to computerised bibliographic services. Their ultimate goal is to provide full text, online retrieval. As these trends continue, the computer centre and the library will actually merge into a single, automated information utility. Regional and national networks will provide scholars with access to information and computational resources anywhere in the country EDUCOM, a nation-wide consortium of universities and colleges, has been developing this concept for several years and now offers its members access to EDUNET, a nationwide resource-sharing data communication network.

**Instructional Management and Administration**

Information technology can be used by the teacher to help plan course work and manage the classroom. Computers not only assist with mundane daily tasks such as grading and record keeping but can also help keep closer track of the daily accomplishments and problems of individual students. Teacher attention can, thus, be more focussed on individual student needs. Teleconferencing via radio, television, or computer allows teachers to exchange experiences, develop curricula, and coordinate educational programmes among a number of schools.

**Distribution Services**

The distribution of services to those who need them has always been a difficult problem, for the educational system for as long as education has been provided by schools, the distribution problem has been responsible for institutional constraints of both time and location on the student. That schooling takes place on a physical campus, attended principally by young people, may be more reflective of the limitations of the traditional schooling system than it is of the current needs of society for education.

In the past, television and radio have been used for distribution purpose, often to good effect. Information technology is a tool that can address these to distributional problems—distance and time. However, their applicability has been limited both by the need to use expensive and rare broadcast facilities to serve a relatively small clientele and by the inability to provide interactive services. Modern technology removes these barriers.

Communication facilities such as cable, direct broadcast

sattellite, low-power television, and video cassette and video disk will greatly increase the number of information channels coming into the home and office. Two-way cable, remote conferencing facilities, and optical video disk microcomputer systems provide the capability for interactive education.

The particular applications of information technology for distribution are the following:

1. *General educational services to dispersed populations:* Some geographical regions need to provide schooling to a sparse population spread over a large area. Communications technology such as direct broadcast sattellite or low power television allows educational programming to be broadcast at low cost to small rural communities and even to individual residences. Video cassettes, video disks, and personal computer programmes can be distributed physically by mail.
2. *Specialised educational services to small populations:* Some groups in society that have very specialised needs for educational services are not concentrated geographically. Only by providing courses regionally or nationally can a critical mass of students be assembled to justify the expense of the course. Information: systems provide that wider market. For example:
   (a) Instruction in subjects for which experienced teachers are scarce or courses conducted by outstanding scholars and leaders in a field.
   (b) Advanced professional training, especially continuing education in such fields as medicine, law, and engineering, in which knowledge advances at a rapid rate.
   (c) Unusual educational needs, such as accelerated-science programmes for the gifted or courses conducted in a foreign language.

4. *Job-related education and training in the workplace:* There are a number of barriers to workers who wish to take job-related instruction. Attending regular classes is difficult due to competing demands on their time, travel to a campus may be burdensome, and there is reluctance on the part of some order individuals to sit in a classroom and compete with younger students. Information technology, by bringing the course to the workplace, can remove some of these constraints.
4. *Education for the homebound*: For a number of reasons—e.g., illness, physical handicap, or age—many individuals in society cannot travel physically to attend a class. Information technology can provide educational services directly to the home, hospital, or workplace.

**Testing and Diagnosis**

Computers have been used for some time to grade and analyse the results of college admission exams, intelligence tests, and a variety of psychometric examinations designed to explore the values, attitudes, and thinking patterns of individuals. Educational testing can be thought of as having four basic roles:

1. *Tactical:* Testing also takes place during instructional sequences to determine how the student is progressing through the course and to detect and diagnose difficulties the student might be having.
2. *Gatekeeping:* Testing plays an increasingly important role in supporting decisions to institutions and to programmes of study. It is a basis for allocating scarce-resources (e.g. admission to a prestigious college or university) and for the granting of licenses to practice professions.
3. *Strategic:* Testing helps assess a student's general levels of understanding and learning strategies. It is

used to determine what classes and courses of study a student should pursue, and what instructional approaches would be most effective for him. After a course, testing measures the skills and knowledge that the student.

4. *Certification:* Testing plays an important role in certifying the knowledge and skill of individuals, qualifying them to pursue professions such as medicine or law, or attesting that they have progressed along certain educational or training peths.

Modern information technology will likely have several effects on testing:

1. Automated teaching systems depend on continual testing and evaluation to direct the presentation of material.
2. Continual testing of students' progress and levels of understanding is an important pedagogical tool, even in a nonautomated teaching environment. However it is very demanding of a teacher's time. Automated systems will allow much closer monitoring of student and class progress in a normal classroom environment.
3. Automated instruction may lead to a decoupling of instruction from institutions—in the sense that a student moves freely between home, job, and school for coursework. This trend will create greater need for strategic testing to determine appropriate instructional programmes for students.
4. The accelerating growth of knowledge is pressuring professions such as medicine, law, and engineering to require retraining and periodic renewal of certifications.

5. Institutional decoupling will also require more testing for purposes of certification. Traditionally, an engineering degree was obtained by following a course of study at one department. Certification was the degree earned by successfully completing the programme.
6. If traditional forms of education become increasingly extensive and, hence, scarce, gatekeeping requirements will inevitably continue to grow in importance. The current competition for entry into medical school illustrates this trend.
7. On the other hand, automated learning systems may make certain types of education and training far more accessible and affordable. If that occurs, gatekeeping may take place not on entry to the education programme, but in licensing to practice.

## Capabilities of Educational Technology

None of the technologies and services overview has the capabilities required to support all of the applications listed above. Hence, the growth of an extensive automated education network will depend on the integration of information technologies.

Each particular technology—cable, personal computers, etc.—has some but not all of the capabilities necessary to provide effective education. Thus, the basic message is that different information technologies will need to be linked in order to provide all of the capabilities needed for extensive automated learning systems to be developed.

## Cost and Effectiveness

For a long time the cost and effectiveness of educational technology has served to circumscribe the debate about whether and how it should be used. OTA found that:

> There is a substantial amount of agreement that, for many educational applications, information technology can be an effective and economical tool for instruction.

This conclusion is based on a number of observations including:

1. Research exists, some of it dating back years, to suggest that students do learn as well or better from educational technology than from convential means. Little evidence exists to the contrary. Much of the past debate centered around whether technology was more effective than conventional means and hence warranted substitution for traditional classroom instruction.
2. Costs for labour-intensive education and training methods continue to climb faster than the inflation rate, while costs for information technology continue to drop precipitously. These trends will result in a steadily growing number of applications in which technology-based instruction is clearly the most-effective method.
3. For many educational and training needs—e.g., educational services to the homebound, to geographically isolated regions, or to the workplace—there are few viable alternatives to the use of technology, provided that it works adequately. In a growing number of instances, teachers qualified to teach in certain fields—such as science, mathematics, or bilingual education are difficult to find. In these cases, technology may be the only means by which such education can be provided.

This is not to say that there are no potential limitations or dangers in the uncritical use of educational technology nor that there is no need for additional research in the field. In fact, in the eyes of some critics, a number of questions remain unanswered.

1. If, over the long term, education is provided principally by technology, what are the unintented long-term impacts on social, cognitive, and psychological development ? Very few answers to this important question are known. However, since it would take several years before technological and institutional changes could create such a possibility on a massive scale, there seems to be adequate time to study it.
2. Will access to computers reduce the ability to practice and learn basic skills? Some parents and teachers are concerned that student use of hand calculators may lead to the atrophy of simple computational skills. Some modern word processors incorporate spelling correction facilities, and now many systems incorporate simple grammatical analysis and correction. Will use of such technology decrease a student's grasp of writing mechanisms?
3. Most research on technology-based education has focused on the development of well defined skills, such as arithmetic computation or foreign-language vocabulary. While proponents argue that computers can encourage the development of new problem-solving skills, critics suggest that education of the more general conceptual skills could suffer.
4. Does the medium have characteristics that, when exploited, distort the educational message or produce subtle side effects? Some observers, for example, have suggested that television educational programmes such as Sesame Street may reinforce short attention spans. A similar example is the finding

of some developers of interactive computer based reading programmes that, in order to maintain student attention, shorter passages must be used on video screens than would be needed to maintain student attention for reading exercises on paper.

5. Do particular characteristics of information technology subtle favour some types of students psychologically or cognitively? Do differences exist that tend to favour performance by sex, age, social class, or values? These questions are important when dealing with issues of social equity.

**Learning Resources**

Knowledgeable in the field of technology, people whether they work in education or not, would probably agree that the use of technology in the profession of teaching and learning has not reached its true potential. While external reasons for this apparent non-achievement of potential are numerous, few organisations have looked at internal adjustments as avenues for achieving a higher level performance. A point of view on this subject that is seldom articulated or addressed suggests that each time a new technological breakthrough occurs, it is too often viewed as a separate and isolated entity and offered as a cure for all the existing educational ills. For this reason the positive impact of combining and integrating educational support technologies has seldom, if ever, been realised.

Generally speaking, current higher education practice finds that each of these technologies is utilised with only a remote awareness of the possibilities for positive interaction with the others. Library, audiovisual, television, instructional, development, message design, telecommunications, interactive video, computer-assisted instruction—all these terms are familiar to everyone working in higher education. Standing alone, each is built on a substantial body of knowledge; each creates its own set of utilisation and administrative problems. This interaction is the thrust of the learning resources organisation an organisation that merits further investigation and analysis by higher education.

The learning resources services (LRS) model makes it possible to combine the strengths of the appropriate technologies to be applied to the solution of teaching and leaning problems. Here, we examine how one university has, during the last many years, attempted to implement the definition of instructional technology that was reported in the 1970 statement of the Commission on Instructional Technology:

> instructional technology goes beyond any particular medium or device. In this sense, instructional technology is more than the sum of its parts. It is a systematic way of designing, carrying out, and evaluating the total process-of learning and teaching in terms of specific objectives, based on research in human learning and communication and employing a combination of human and nonhuman resources to bring about more effective instruction. The widespread acceptance and application of this broad definition belongs to the future. Though only a limited number of institutions have attempted to design instruction using such a systematic comprehensive approach, there is reason to believe that this approach holds the key to the contribution technology can make to the advancement of education.

The LRS model has five programme elements.

(a) Human resources,

(b) Instructional materials,

(c) Instructional equipment,

(d) Preparation of the Information Specialist, and

(e) Programme costs.

## Human Resources

The human resources element in any organisation creates many complex problems and challenges. So it follows that the most important tasks within the human resources element of the LRS model are hiring, assignment or placement of personnel, and development of personnel. Faculty entering the organisation must possess a broad background. Academic preparation in library science, audiovisual education, and instructional development is required. The degree may be in any one of the disciplines, but preparation in several others will be required before tenure is granted. For example, a person entering the organisation with a master's degree in library science must have in addition a required number of credits in instructional technology. All of the professional personnel are academically prepared to address service questions from the broadcast possible perspective, for the learning resources concept does not establish a hierarchy among the media.

Higher education with its traditional print orientation has been challenged to face information and communication problems without the prejudice that one medium has greater validity than another. It is the responsibility of LRS personnel to provide direction to this important information age challenge. The most successful persons will be specialists able to adapt to changing situations, and they will flexible and constantly motivated and challenged by the service needs of the user.

New candidates must be carefully screened so that the emerging needs are addressed. The change in the discipline and practice covered within LRS concept requires retraining, since LRS faculty and staff turnover is not as rapid as the change occurring within the associated technologies. Professional development programmes clearly be related to current trends. Given the need for objective measurement, academic evaluation, and professional development, the personal characteristics of the media professional should not be over-looked. The growth of information combined with changes in communication systems complex LRS faculty and staff to be adaptable, creative, and flexible in their approach to service.

The art of combining a portion of the two most rapidly growing industries in the United States (Porat, 1977)—information and service—and sharing these advances with university faculty and students is indeed a challenge. Today most institutions of higher education have some people using the newer technologies in isolated situations, but few have a group of dedicated persons organised for the sole purpose of providing resources for learning based on the broadcast perspective. LRS faculty and staff can provide a university with some assurance that all the resources and technology available within the budget constraints of that institution wilt be utilised to the fullest potential. Any description of the human aspects is not complete without some discussion of the interchange necessary among faculty, staff, and users.

The utilisation of technology necessitates the development of "user friendly" equipment and procedures or routines. Staff assignments within learning, resources are shifting away from backroom cataloging and similar support activities to a higher level of interaction with, users. Consequently, job descriptions and recruiting emphases must reflect the changing service responsibilities everywhere.

**Instructional Materials**

Traditional formulas for library budgets have been used to evaluate the adequacy and quality of collections, but the newer technologies have not been incorporated in the assessment. The most often used measure of the quality of a collection is still quantity, that is of counting volumes or things. This method certainly has some value, especially in the research library, as most information today continues to be stored and retrieved via the book. Its pervasive application, however, in higher education settings provides a cause for concern. Efforts should be made to use technology-based systems to assess how well the users needs are being fulfilled. This will allow for the development of libraries on the basis of need rather than current quantitative standards.

The periodical collection offers unique opportunities for cost-effective change without a deterioration in service. Communication systems assure availability of articles from a periodicals that may then be dropped from a collection as a paper subscription. The displacement of a paper subscription (near and dear to the heart of some professors, who feel that no self-respecting library would be without one), even if it is unused, creates frustration and tension. This stress can be eased by the assurance that resource needs will be met; the confidence can be developed when appropriate services are provided in a timely manner.

One more important consideration in bringing information to persons in a cost-effective manner concerns departmental ownership. Sometimes services should and must, be duplicated; but in such instances, clearly defined, functional needs should be articulated. The right of a faculty member in a department to have his or her learning resources needs met is paramount; however, the manner in which such needs are met should not be his or her decision alone. Competing and equally important needs in departments and agencies within the university must also be considered. For example, certain materials and equipment are useful only to certain departments, but a great many are seldom used and can be shared. How this sharing can be effectively and efficiently accomplished is the continuing challenge of LRS. A goal of all educational institutions is the improvement of instruction so that learning by students will always be at the optimal level.

To reach this goal, most universities will provide some level of instructional development. The LRS model provides a preferred location for developers to reside administratively, since books, films, videotapes, and so forth generally provide some of the needed background information. The model facilitates the interactions of the developer with the appropriate university faculty and the materials collections. It promotes instructional development as a continuous process with the goal of improving teaching through systematic planning and communication. A university faculty person entering any part of the system will be referred to the level of service and support most likely to fulfil his or her needs. Requests that can be effectively and efficiently accommodated by the LRS model are those involving the production of instructional materials. Materials relating to content are easily retrieved from any one of the university owned collections. Further, the person managing such a collection may become a member of the production team. Collection development is also enhanced because weakness in the collections are often identified during the process of production.

### Instructional Equipment

LRS model's key element is the acquisition and distribution of the instructional equipment. An online inventory provides current status information on all university owned instructional equipment. A computer-based maintenance, scheduling, and monitoring package assists in keeping the equipment serviceable and also provides information for future use. Practical cost-effective equipment is acquired, because useful background information is available for decision making. All the components mentioned above must be present to make a centralised distribution system successful, but the system will still fail without the services of a LRS professional to negotiate and identify the functions that the equipment is expected to fulfil. Faculty and student needs must be served in a perceptive, non-judgemental manner. The ability to say no to a request for a certain brand of equipment but at the same time show how the needed functions can be addressed is essential to the success of the programme.

**Preparation of Information Specialists**

An instructional programme that prepares persons to become-information specialists is readily accommodated by the LRS model. Graduates from this programme enter careers in schools, government, public libraries, business, and industry. The teaching unit supports its own faculty based on full-time equivalent (FTE) production. These FTE positions are utilised in such a manner that the expertise of the entire LRS professional staff is available as needed. This ensures that students will be able to acquire both breadth and depth of content and experience in completion of their studies. A. practicing cataloger teaches cataloging, a television producer teaches the television production class, and so on. In addition to the availability of quality faculty, accessibility to the university's information, production, and communications equipment is also assured. The students are able to interact with, the types of systems they are studying in the classroom. Professional production capabilities, along with the latest technologies are available for instruction and exploration.

**Programme Costs**

Empirical evidence seems to indicate that expenditures for staff, equipment, and materials compare favourably with other models in institutions of similar size and scope. Comparisons of book, equipment, periodical, and personnel budgets over the past five years show that monetary outlays fall below that of comparable universities. On the other hand, service is rated high by the users as well as by outside evaluators. It is fair to generalise that the various services addressed in this paper bear similar costs to those located in different settings. Therefore, the sharing factor in the areas of faculty, equipment, and facilities seems to be providing a significant bonus to the campus community.

**Summary**

Professional associations and organisations, along with educational institutions, have acclaimed the wonders of the of the new technology only to find that their early hopes for it were probably too optimistic. A statement attributed to Benjamin Franklin rings true. He said, "Human happiness is produced not so much by great pieces of good fortune that seldom happen, as by little advantages that occur every day." LRS faculty and staff can provide superior service through the identification and use of those "little advantages." The fact that this learning resources model provides a larger base from which creative projects can be launched is such an advantage. The model also provides for physical and organisational proximity, which should provide for better communication and as, a result, better service. In addition, partnership with other institutions in the community and with business and industry are enhanced. An organisation designed to acquire and share learning resources for a campus is well equipped to develop partnerships beyond the confines of the university. This type of service, however, requires some centralisation of budget, which of course is anathema to some. Centralisation should and indeed must occur until the ability to serve is reduced because of it.

The establishment of this five line between centralisation and decentralisation may well be the most critical undertaking in the establishment and operation of a LRS model. The entire faculty and staff must be involved in the drawing of that line; even while it is being drawn, forces are at work that may well affect the scope and breadth of that line. This is the nature of service. Information specialists should be challenged by the changing needs of the users and try to meet them on a continuing basis. They must avoid the human urge to protect the more comfortable ways of the past when they obstruct the path of the present or the future. This should not be misconstrued as an attempt to show disrespect for past efforts; instead, it is an attempt to address the future in a positive manner.

Not all universities can or should do exactly what this university has done. Each institution must address its resource problems in light of its own mission, but it is hoped that the idea of sharing the unused, the unknown, and the unidentified resources can be addressed in some way on every university campus. LRS is not a place; it is a programme composed of people and equipment and collections. All of the components of this programme exist on every campus. It is the responsibility of the administration at each campus to blend them in the most productive manner.

## REFERENCES

Commission on Instructional Technology, (1970). *To Improve Learning, A Report to the President and the Congress of the United States* (Syst. of Docs. Y4. ED 8/1: L47). Washington, DC: U.S. Government Printing Office.

Porat, M. (1977). *The Information Economy: Definition and Measurement* (Office of Telecommunications Special Publication 77-12 [1]). Washington, DC: U.S. Government Printing Office.

# 3

# Educational Technology: Scope and Meaning

Since the dawn of civilisation, before man learnt to speak, he felt the need for communicating his ideas and thoughts to other men. For this he adopted various signs and symbols. He used movements of his hands, legs and other parts of the body to convey different messages. Gradually man learnt to convey his thoughts through this method. Movements of the parts of the body were associated with common meanings understood by all men. Even now we sometimes use this method called the body language to convey our thoughts.

*Conveying Thought Before Men Learnt to Speak*

Next, man learnt to make articulated sounds which he could repeat. He associated one kind of sound with one object and repeated the same sound whenever he referred to that object. This was the origin of words and of language. Even today a mother teaches her young child the use of words in this way. When a word is spoken while a particular object is seen or shown, the sound of the word is associated with that object. After such repeated association, by merely uttering the word without showing the object, the meaning of the object is conveyed; that is, in the mind a mental image of the object is formed when the word is spoken. Gradually, man developed his vocabulary, i.e., learnt more and more words; he coined newer and newer words to signify objects, their qualities, actions and qualities of actions etc. Body language was no longer necessary; he could convey his messages more clearly and accurately through spoken words.

*Learning the Use of Words*

Man's ability to speak and use words meaningfully was the most important factor responsible for his mental development. Using this ability to use words, man acquired more knowledge and ability to use knowledge. Man developed memory. He could express his experiences in words which had equivalent mental images which could be stored in memory.

This was his knowledge which he could reproduce whenever needed. Not only did he gain knowledge from his own experiences but he also gained knowledge when he heard of the experiences of others. Knowledge added more to his previous knowledge. He could establish different relationships between new and old knowledge, such as, bigger, smaller, same, opposite, etc. By establishing linkages with previous knowledge, man developed more complex forms of knowledge. However, before he learnt to write, man stored his knowledge in his memory and passed on his knowledge to other men by speaking to them, asking them to repeat until they could store them in their memory and reproduce at will.

*Acquiring Knowledge*

Man was able to acquire more and more knowledge from his experiences as well as from experiences of others which were told to him with the development of language and his ability to speak and remember. Older men who had acquired a lot of knowledge passed on their knowledge to younger men by speaking to them and asking them to repeat until they could retain them in their memory. These younger men added on more knowledge as they grew older and again passed on their knowledge to the next generation. Thus knowledge passed on from generation to generation through the use of spoken words while continuously increasing in this process.

### Earliest Methods of Teaching

First organised teaching and learning began with man's desire to pass on his accumulated knowledge to younger men so that this knowledge was preserved, further developed and passed on from generation to generation. Some people called Gurus or teachers specialised in acquiring knowledge and repeating them so that they always remembered them. Each of them took a few younger people as *shisyas* or students to whom they gave their knowledge through spoken words. The students repeated this knowledge until they could remember and reproduce at will. The *Guru* not only gave the *shisyas* knowledge but related this knowledge to their individual and social conduct, thereby influencing their conduct and behaviour. In India the earliest form of knowledge is known as *Sruti,* that is, that which is heard, because this was passed on from *Guru* to *shisya* by hearing from the *Guru.*

As knowledge grew, it became very difficult for one person to remember all the knowledge and to pass on all of it to the next generation by spoken words. A temporary solution was found by suitably classifying and dividing knowledge so that one person remembered knowledge of one category while another remembered knowledge of another category. But with further growth to knowledge, even this method was not very satisfactory. Man's capacity to remember knowledge put a limit to his knowledge and ability to acquire and use more knowledge. Man therefore searched for a method of recording knowledge. By making scratches on stone, wood, leather and some dry leaves, man was able to draw outlines of objects and other symbols to denote particular objects.

Gradually he developed the use of written symbols to convey some meanings. Thus developed the figurative script still being used in China and Japan. Elsewhere symbols were used for particular sounds and alphabetical scripts developed. Using such scripts, man was able to record knowledge on leather and dry leaves. In India, a lot of old recorded knowledge is still available on dry palm leaves.

*Knowledge Recording: Earliest Method*

**Effect of Printed Books**

Writing on leather and on dry leaves was not an easy task, so man was on the lookout for a better material to write on. His knowledge about nature and natural materials grew and he established this knowledge on a rational systematic basis and called it science. He was able to prepare new materials by mixing different substances and sometimes by application of hear. In this way, he learnt to prepare wood-pulp, spread it thin over a plane surface and dry it, thus obtaining paper, a white smooth surface on which he could easily write. He prepared a black liquid called ink with the help of which he could write on paper. He also found that he could write with carbon or graphite on paper and prepared pencils using thin strips of graphite. Since paper was made out of wood-pulp and there was no scarcity of wood, paper could be prepared in large quantities and people began writing on it to preserve knowledge. The teacher as well as students had access to much larger amounts of knowledge than they could store in their memory. This was the time when Europe had the industrial revolution. Various kinds of machines were being invented and among them was the printing press which brought revolutionary changes in man's knowledge and its spread. Formerly knowledge was restricted to a few individuals who could learn it from a teacher by memorisation. Now the printing press could record knowledge on paper and make as many copies as needed. This led to publication of large numbers of copies of books. Any person could buy a book, read it and obtain knowledge. The teacher was no longer the only storehouse of knowledge. The books became larger and better storehouses of knowledge and were accessible to a much larger number of people. Students obtained knowledge not only from the teacher but also from books. The teacher lost, to some extent, his pre-eminent position in the teaching-learning process and some of his functions were taken over by books. The printing press thus marked the earliest advent of technology into education.

*The Earliest Advent of Technology into Education*

While the printed book performed some functions of the teacher, the teacher did not feel threatened by its presence. The teacher knew that the book could not replace him; it could only supplement what he did, by providing more information and storing information for future reference. Particularly in the earlier stages of education, the teacher's role is essential in developing the language ability of the child to enable it to use a book profitably. Only after a child's language abilities are sufficiently well developed, can he read and understand a book without the Help of a teacher. Further the child should also have the prerequisite knowledge based on which the book is written. Books on any branch of knowledge can be graded; those giving knowledge of higher level are based on some prerequisite knowledge which are given in other books. Even though the child has the requisite language abilities and prerequisite knowledge on which the contents of the book are based, he may still not understand the book unless the presentation of contents of the book is such that he can understand without the help of a teacher. Such a style of presentation is called 'self-instruction style'. In such a style, the author presents matter in the book in the manner of a teacher teaching a pupil; that is, having analysed the topic, leading the reader gradually by small steps from simple to complex, reinforcing learning at every step. Thus, we may say that a reader can read and understand a book without the help of a teacher provided:

(i) he has necessary language competence,
(ii) he has the prerequisite knowledge of the subject of the book,
(iii) the presentation of the book is such that he can understand by self-study.

On the other hand, the teacher learnt to make the best use of the printed book for the teaching-learning process. He graded the books, asked pupils to read the books he recommended, explained and elaborated the contents of the books, interlinked contents of several books and used the contents of the book for evaluation of learning. The teacher thus used the book as a valuable aid in teaching. The pupil also found the book useful when it was explained by the teacher and used in the teaching-learning process.

*Use of Book as an Teaching Aid*

The medium of instruction of both the teacher and the printed book was 'words'. How did man learn the use of words in his early childhood? A word was used to signifiy an object seen by the child. Meanings of words were made clear by giving the child appropriate experiences using his sense organs of sight, hearing, touch, smell and taste. These are the five gateways of acquiring experiences. Words are used to name particular experiences, so that a word evokes in the mind the mental image of the experience associated with the word. Two persons will have the same meaning of a word to the extent to which they have the same experiences associated with the word.

*When does a Word Mean the Samething to Two Persons?*

The teacher may have seen a camel, but the students may

not have seen it. So when the teacher uses the word 'camel', the student who has not seen it cannot construct a mental image of the camel. The teacher may use other words to describe it. Yet each student will develop a different mental image. If the teacher can show a camel to all the students, the meaning of the word 'camel' will be the same for all students. So in order to give common experiences to all students, the teacher shows the real objects about which he teaches. When he cannot bring the objects to the classroom, he takes the students out to show them. Thus he takes them to places of historical interest while teaching history and to other places to study nature and natural objects etc.

## Development of Audiovisual Aids

Sometimes it is neither possible for the teacher to bring the object to the class nor to take the class to the object. In such a case, the teacher shows an object which is very much similar to it. A model of the object is prepared in the likeness of the object except for the size—sometimes smaller, sometimes larger than the object. By showing the model and explaining the relationship of the model to the object, the teacher can develop a common mental picture of the object in the minds of the students.

The real object or model gives a three-dimensional visual experience. Also the students can gain further experience by touching it. When the teacher can neither show the object nor a model of it, he tries to show a picture of the object. He may show ' a painting of the object, a drawing on the blackboard, or what is better, a photograph. The photograph is another application of technology in education. The invention of the camera and the chemical process of developing and printing of photographs, enabled the teacher to use photographs as aids in teaching. Using technology he can also prepare filmstrips and slides which he can use in projectors to obtain an enlarged image of the photograph to be shown to all students. The invention of the movie camera added movement to the pictures, so that it was possible for him to photograph and show action through photographs. All these are called visual aids to instruction, as the teacher uses them as teaching aids to give common visual experiences to the students.

*Visual Aids to Instruction*

The invention of the phonograph is another milestone in the application of technology to education. It is now possible to record sound in discs and reproduce it at will. Other methods of recording and reproducing sound were also invented—namely, optical recording of sound on the film and the magnetic recording of sound on magnetic tapes and cassettes. All these inventions have many educational uses. The teacher can use them very effectively in the teaching of language, social studies and music. Good music recorded on discs, tapes or cassettes can be played back any number of times to develop appreciation of music as well as to learn to sing. As the child learns to sing or play a musical instrument, it can also be recorded and played back so that the child can detect his mistakes and rectify them. The language teacher can use the record player and tape recorder in teaching correct pronunciation as well as correct speaking. Phonetic records are now available which can be played as many times as required and the student asked to speak exactly as recorded. In this way the student can learn correct pronunciation. As the student learns the language, his own voice can be recorded and played back and his mistakes pointed out to him. Not only can the child learn the mother tongue in this way but he can also learn a foreign language. In social studies and other subjects, we can record speeches of great men and reproduce them whenever we want, even after they are dead. Thus we can still hear the recorded voices of leaders like Mahatma Gandhi and Sardar Patel—what they had said about the problems of India during its struggle for independence. This has great significance in the teaching of Indian history. Record players, tape recorders and cassette recorders are used by the teacher to increase the effectiveness of instruction. These are called audio-aids to instruction.

*Audio Aids to Instruction*

The optical recording of sound on films gave rise to sound-movie films. It became not only possible to photograph men in action and to show their action in pictures but also to record and to reproduce their voices and other sounds associated with their action. Historical episodes can thus be enacted, recorded and reproduced. We can also photograph and record the sound associated with any current event happening in any part of the world and show it as it happened to any audience anywhere in the world. The films can also be shown projected on a large screen so that a large audience can see them at the same time. The sound-movie film not only became an effective medium of entertainment but also an effective medium of education. When used by the teacher to illustrate and show clearly events about which he is teaching, it may be called an audiovisual aid to instruction. Sometimes, however, the sound-movie film can be projected and shown to an audience without any teacher doing any teaching. The film itself when projected gives some instruction to the audience. As such we call the film a 'medium of instruction' rather than a 'teaching-aid' or 'aid to instruction'. In the same way the recorded audio tape or cassette can also be used by the student himself for self-learning without the teacher. In that case also it is a medium of instruction rather than a teaching aid. A medium of instruction is thus a method of communication by which instruction can be imparted by itself alone. These are also called 'mass media', since these can address to a large number of people at a time. The printed book can also be considered a medium of instruction, and the newspapers, periodicals and journals are mass media.

## Effect of Radio and Television on Education

The radio and the television are the two powerful mass media that were later invented and are extensively used today. Although these two media are predominantly used for propagation of news and for entertainment, much of the information that is propagated has educational implication. Further, during the recent years, special educational programmes meant for targetted audience have been broadcast at scheduled times through the radio and television. These are listened to or seen and listened to by the targetted audience. A coordinator collects the responses of the targetted audience and arranges remedial instructions again through radio and television. Sometimes the broadcasts are supplemented by printed matter and/or recorded audio/video tapes sent by mail. Thus multimedia packages of instruction are developed and used for particular groups for specific objectives. Such a method of imparting education through mass media to large targetted groups spread over large distance is called 'distance education.'

## Programmed Learning and Teaching Machines

During the middle of the twentieth century, a new method of instruction called 'Programmed Learning' was discovered. This is a method of individualised self-instruction, where each individual learns by himself at his own rate. Keeping in view the educational objectives, the educational content is broken up into smaller elements which are arranged in a sequence in such a way that a student can easily learn by himself. The new knowledge is broken up into small elements called 'steps'. These steps are arranged in a sequence in such a way that the knowledge given in one step is based on the knowledge given in the previous step. Each step contains a question, the answer to which can be obtained from the knowledge given in the previous step(s). After writing the answer to the question in each step, the student can compare it with the correct answer given therein. If his answer is correct, he proceeds to the next step; otherwise he studies the previous step again. Briefly this is programmed learning. We shall discuss this later in greater detail.

Programmed learning is also called Programmed Instruction. There are two ways in which programmed instruction is presented to the student. The simplest way is to present it in the form of a printed book. A programmed text differs from an ordinary textbook in the way in which the knowledge is presented. In the programmed text, the new knowledge is presented in small sequential steps, each step containing a question, the answer to which can be found from the knowledge in the previous step. The student is expected to write his response to each question and then compare it with the correct answer given in the text (usually at the bottom of the page). If he is correct, he proceeds on to the next step, otherwise he re-reads the previous step and tries to understand the correct answer. In this manner, he learns by himself at his own rate. No teacher is necessary in this process.

Programmed instruction can also be presented through teaching machines. A teaching machine is a device which allows the student to see one step of the programme at a time. He has then to indicate his response by a selection of buttons or operating a keyboard. If his response is correct, he can see the next step of the programme. Otherwise he has to read again the previous step and try to find the correct response. In this way, the student learns by operating the machine himself. He does not need the assistance of the teacher. Only one student will operate a machine at a time. So we need as many machines as the number of students who would learn simultaneously. However more than one student can use the same machine by time sharing.

## Use of Computer in Education

The latest gift of technology to mankind which is also used in education is the computer. The computer is an automatic electronic machine which can process very quickly coded information according to rules or instructions fed into the machine. There are four basic elements in the computer; the input, the processor, the storage (or memory) and the output. Instructions to the machine are called 'Programmes' and are in coded language and developed by specialists called programmers. These are fed into the computer through the input and stored in the storage (or memory). The computer can store several programmes in its memory and any one can be called back on request through the input. The input is usually a type writer keyboard console. The request when typed is either typed on a roll of paper or displayed on a cathode ray tube. The computer recalls the appropriate programme on request indicated through input. The processor processes the input according to the programme and the result is exhibited in the output; that is, it is typed on the roll of paper or displayed on the cathode ray tube.

*Four Basic Elements of a Computer*

The computer can be used in many ways in education. In its simplest form, programmed instruction can be stored in it and a student can interact with it in almost the same way as with a teaching machine. However, more complicated programmes can be fed into the computer so that it can evaluate a pupil's response, diagnose his difficulty and present remedial materials until the pupil can find the correct answer. It can also be used in computing, in finding solutions to problems, in simulating hypothetical conditions and finding consequences, etc. Using the computer in this way is called Computer Assisted Learning (CAL). The computer can also be used for management of learning when it is called Computer

Managed Learning (CML). In this case, it is used for assessment of students' answers, record keeping and reporting.

*Two Basic Ways of Using the Computer in Education*

In the foregoing pages a historical development of the application of technology to education has been briefly presented. While in the beginning, education was imparted wholly by the teacher through his talk, we have now come to a stage when education can be imparted wholly through technology, although educational personnel are still needed to develop the educational material to be presented through technology. Between these two extreme positions, we have a large range in which both teacher and technology work together in the process of education. Sometimes, the teacher resents the use of technology in education, perhaps because he thinks of technology as a competitor which may completely eliminate him from education. This fear is justified to some extent, since in some cases education can be imparted through technology without the teacher.

*Teachers Resenting Use of Technology in Education*

Can technology completely eliminate the teacher from education? Although technology can do a number of teaching functions quite effectively, there will still be a place for the teacher in education. In the first place he determines the objectives of education and plans an educational system which can achieve the objectives. He develops the appropriate educational content and determines the process by which the content is to be conveyed to the students. He monitors the progress of the students and keeps record of the same either manually or through technology. He evaluates the achievement of students with reference to the objectives and modifies the system if necessary. The teacher or educational personnel will still plan, organise, operate, evaluate and replan the educational system in which technology may play an important part.

*Role of Teacher in a System of Education Where Technology Plays an Important Part*

Some people argue that the use of technology dehumanises education. It diminishes the influence of the personality of the teacher on the students. According to them, only the teacher can shape the personality and character of the students and this cannot be done by technology. There is a fallacy in this argument. For, even when education is imparted through technology, the teacher is very much there. Rather, there may be more than one teacher. In the television lessons, the student is taught by some expert teachers. He listens to some teachers in his radio lessons. Even in the programmed instruction and computer assisted instruction, he is interacting with an invisible teacher who has developed the programmes. These visible and/or invisible teachers who teach him through different media, also have a method of getting feedback from the students and modifying and sending fresh instruction as may be needed to achieve the objectives of education.

*The Use of Technology In education*

Why should we use technology in education? What are the advantages and disadvantages of such use? These are important considerations and should be considered in respect of each application of technology to education. Although these will be discussed in greater detail in the following chapters, a brief discussion is presented here. The traditional method of teaching by the teacher is by using the spoken words. Sometimes he may write these words on the blackboard or ask students questions or ask them to repeat what he says or to write them in their note-books. In other words, he tries to convey his ideas or messages through words. We also know that a word is meaningful to a student if it is associated with his past experience. He may understand the word 'white' if he has seen some white things such as chalk, paper, milk etc. and been told that they are white. But if the teacher says 'pearl-white' only those who have seen a pearl will understand but not others. They will however understand 'pearl-white' if the teacher can show them some pearls or show them something which has colour similar to pearls. Thus showing real objects or giving first-hand experience of the real world becomes necessary in teaching. When the real objects cannot be shown due to their size or inaccessibility or unavailability, we show replicas of the same three-dimensional models or two-dimensional pictures. To show action of these objects, we can show working models or movie pictures and sound-motion pictures. Description of a game unfamiliar to students by means of words will not be meaningful; but an actual demonstration of the game will be quite meaningful. It will also be almost equally meaningful, if a sound-motion picture of the game is shown. Thus audiovisual aids to instruction are absolutely necessary for good teaching as they provide suitable sensory experience to make words meaningful. The audiovisual aids increase the cost of education. They also increase instruction time. As such, only those audiovisual aids which are necessary should be used.

### *Advantages and Disadvantages of Using Audio-visual Aids*

What are the advantages and disadvantages of using mass media such as radio and television for education? One advantage is that the radio and television lessons can be developed and presented by very competent educators and presenters and the advantage of listening to good teaching can be had even in rural areas. Through these media, it is possible to educate very large groups of people in a very short time. The television has the added advantage of showing events that happened in distant places, around the world. Scientific experiments conducted in special laboratories, which cannot be performed in the ordinary school laboratory, can be shown through television. Radio and television can also be very effectively used for teaching of foreign languages.

For more practice and drill in a foreign language, the student can use recorded audio/video tapes which he can play back. The disadvantage is that the initial cost of equipment and programme production of mass media system of education is very high, although in the long run, the per pupil cost turns out to be lower than that of traditional education.

*Advantages of Education Through Radio and Television*

How is programmed learning useful in education? In the traditional method of classroom instruction, we group children in standards on the basis of an examination assuming that all those who obtain above a certain mark or grade, belong to one standard. We prescribe a uniform syllabus for all of them and teach them in the same manner assuming that all of them have equal ability to understand. However, we know that there are large individual differences in intelligence, aptitudes and interests and so all children in the class cannot learn to the same extent in the same time. At the end of an academic year, we give them an examination in all subjects taught and 'fail' those who cannot get the required mark or grade for promotion to the next class. Are we justified in expecting all children in the class to learn at the same rate and reach the same level of achievement at the end of the year? The failed student might have done his best but failed to make the grade because he cannot learn as fast as his other classmates. The traditional method of teaching ignores individual differences and penalises students for no fault of theirs. Programmed learning has the advantage that learning is completely individualised. It provides for different rates of learning of different individuals. It provides learning materials suited to each student's ability to learn. It does not 'fail' any student at any time; it can only state the progress made by a student at any time in any subject of study. Thus programmed learning avoids all the drawbacks of traditional teaching and is a psychologically sound method of providing instruction. The disadvantages of using programmed learning are that programmed texts are usually very bulky and the cost of production of these texts in all subjects at different levels is very high. We need a different method of monitoring and guiding a pupil's progress and maintaining records of the same. If teaching machines are used, we need large numbers of them and the initial cost of providing these machines will be very high. However, recurring costs will not be high.

*Advantages of Using Programmed Learning*

What are the advantages of using computers in education? Firstly, in the modern scientific age, computers are likely to be used extensively in industry, in government and also in domestic life. As such, the students of today need to know what a computer can do and how he can use it to his advantage. This means he needs education about the computer. Secondly the computer helps in individualising instruction. In computer assisted learning, suitable educational programmes are developed and stored in the computer's memory. Each student has access to the computer through a computer terminal during a given time. Using the terminal he can interact with the computer and learn the contents of a particular programme. The computer interacts differentially with different students depending on their responses to the questions or information given by the computer. The computer never gets tired nor loses patience and can repeat the information as many times as the student wants. It never forgets the information stored in its memory and never makes mistakes in applying the rules stated in the programme. It is very useful in problem solving, particularly of difficult problems very quickly. It can be used by many students through time sharing. Even students in distant places can have access to it through its terminals. It can also be used for student evaluation, record keeping and reporting. The disadvantages of the computer are that it is still very costly although costs are gradually getting reduced.

Programmes have to be developed or imported which also increase the recurring costs. However after the computers are installed and suitable programmes developed, further recurring costs will be nominal and the advantages will outweigh the disadvantages.

## Meaning of Educational Technology

Having discussed various applications of technology in education, let us now examine what we mean by 'Educational Technology'. Broadly there are three different views of Educational Technology. The first view which we may call $E.T._1$ refers to 'application of technology to instrumentation useful to the process of teaching.' This is the view of Finn and colleagues. The second view which we may call $E.T._2$ refers to 'application of scientific principles to instruction.' This is the view of Skinner, Gagne and others. While $E.T._1$ lays stress on the use of hardware in education, $E.T._2$ emphasises the psychological principles of learning. The modern view of Educational Technology $E.T._3$ as described by Davies and Hartley (1972) 'incorporates both $E.T._1$ and $E.T._2$ through application of a system approach to education and training.' According to this view, education should be considered a system in which men, machines, media and materials are interrelated parts and are organised in such a way that they work together in a pre-planned manner for the fulfilment of specified educational objectives. The system will also incorporate within itself a process of evaluation of the system with reference to the objectives and provide feedback to the planners to review and modify the system. The educational planners, according to this view, should consider the educational objectives, obtain all relevant data about learners, teachers and other personnel, technological devices, machines, media etc., available educational materials and software that can be used by the men, machines or media, and then design a system in which the men, machines, media and materials have their specified roles but are interrelated to one another so that the objectives can be best achieved. As the system works, it is also continuously monitored and evaluated and the feedback given to planners for necessary modification of the system. Educational technology, according to this view, implies planning, implementing and evaluating a system in education according to scientific principles so as to best achieve the educational objectives.

## QUESTIONS

1. Arrange the following in the chronological order of their influence in education: computer, printing press, tape recorder, camera.
2. Name four kinds of visual aids in education.
3. Name the audio-aids used in education.
4. Name the mass media used in education.
5. Name the individualised modes of instruction.
6. Name the advantages of programmed learning.
7. Explain the meaning of educational technology.
8. Describe the role of the teacher in educational technology.
9. How is the computer useful in education?
10. What are the advantages of using programmed learning?
11. How did man convey his thoughts to others before he learnt to speak.
12. How did man learn the use of words?
13. How did human knowledge grow before man learnt writing?

# 4

# Nature and Scope of Educational Technology

The main aim of education is to bring about the all-round development of the personality of the child. The term "all-round development" means two things: (i) individual growth and (ii) social development. Under the label of individual growth are included the child's physical growth, mental growth, intellectual growth and social growth too; whereas under the label of "social development, there is the inclusion of rituals, customs, traditions, culture etc. The following diagrammatic representation will make the fact more clear.

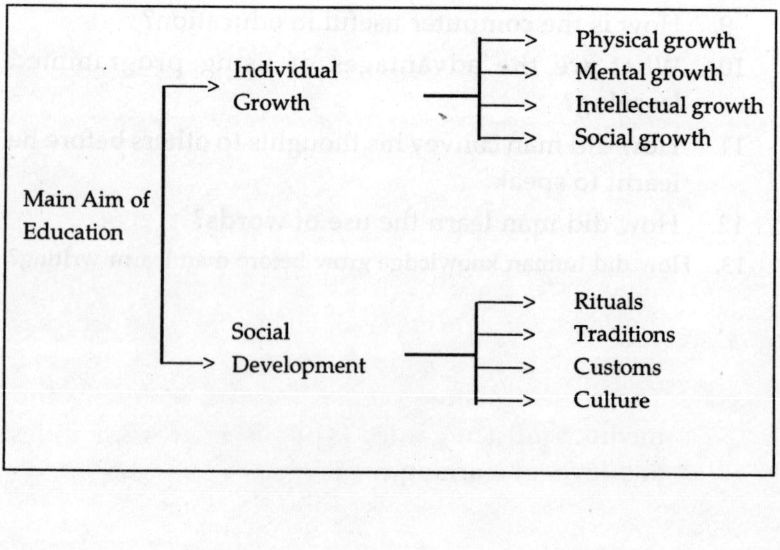

So, in a technical sense, education refers to that process by which society, through its different institutions, deliberately transmits its cultural heritage to its young—its accumulated values, knowledge and skills—from one generation to another.

Education also is an acquired experience of any sort—intellectual, emotional or sensory-motor. Education is a product of experience. It proceeds form birth to death and the agencies that impart education are the school, home, press, radio, television, religion, cinema etc. But life involves constant and continuous modification of experience because attitudes, opinions etc. constantly undergo alterations, and education is that process which helps the child to adjust to this changing world. It is here that technology comes to our help in modernizing the society.

Technology of education is developed with two important aims—the first aim being to make education more widely available and the second being to improve the quality of education that is available.

We have now accepted the fact that today's child is endowed with certain potentialities. He/she has a natural curiosity. Hence pupils should be encouraged to explore, to ask questions, to be creative etc.

On the basis of the abovesaid things, it is also necessary to note certain basic principles of learning which are as follows:

(i) Each pupil is unique and his/her response to any experience will also be unique.

(ii) Perception is the foundation of all learning.

(iii) Unless the learner participates wholeheartedly in the learning process and unless he/she becomes involved, he/she will not learn.

(iv) The subject matter, media learning materials and methods must be graded to puplis' interests, abilities and level of learning readiness.

(v) The teaching strategies adopted must be adequate and appropriate.

(vi) Creativity should be the goal of learning.

(vii) Hence curriculum must be need-based.

Thus, from the above discussions, we can firmly come to the conclusion that education involves learning and that learning is modification of behaviour. This modification of behaviour is the result of past experience. The very basis of learning experiences, that is, the inputs of learning, must reach the pupils. The question, however, is "how"? The answer to this is "Through the senses". For, the senses are the gateways to acquire knowledge. Thus,

| | | |
|---|---|---|
| Learning through | Taste | 1.0% |
| | Touch | 1.5% |
| | Hearing | 11.0% |
| | Smell | 3.5% |
| | Sight | 83.0% |

We remember
- 20% of what we hear
- 30% of what we see
- 50% of what we see & hear
- 80% of what we say
- 90% of what we say & do

Thus, the very basis of learning is sense experience, and the very psychology of teaching aids is as follows:

I hear—I forget

I see—I remember

I do—I learn/understand.

Hence the approach in education must be multi-sensory approach; and this is what educational technology is concerned with.

Education is a three-fold process—imparting knowledge, developing skills and inculcating proper interests, attitudes and life values. But even today, our schools are often mostly concerned with the imparting of knowledge. Today's curriculum is bound to be need-based. As a result of new educational aims, newer methods were designed to foster learning; and educational technology has stimulated teachers to innovate in the areas of school organisation, curriculum construction and teaching methods resulting in newer concepts like "modular scheduling," "team teaching," "self-study project" etc.

From the above discussion, it is clear that educationists have realised the fact that in education "learning" is more important than '"teaching." Learning is concerned with pupils but teaching is concerned with both pupils and teachers. In the very olden days, the very source of knowledge was the teacher. Pupils learnt what the teachers taught. However, with the advent of text-books (i.e., printing) and other teaching aids, the teacher's knowledge though important, ceased to be the only or even the paramount source of learning. Today, the teaching process is not only assisted by the text-book author but by the radio programmer, film producer and many others. The house of education, today, has taken altogether a different shape. The one-way communication of information of the traditional class is no longer effective now in comparison with the modern communication system. The reason for this is nothing but the two important explosions— the knowledge explosion and the population explosion. But these explosions have posed critical problems for education; and have also brought tremendous changes in the developed as well as the developing countries. But it is not possible to solve the problems successfully without the help of varied media of communication, varied types of evaluation, varied ways of modern testing methods etc. Especially in a developing country like India, new/current techniques in the field of education has to be mastered by the educationists if we want to be on par with the developed nations. Hence, the quantitative expansion and also a qualitative expansion, that is, improvement, are very much required which can be attained only with the help of educational technology.

Eric Ashby (1967) has identified four revolutions in education. The first revolution occurred when societies began to differentiate adult roles and the task of educating the young was shifted, in part, from parents to teachers and from the home to the school.

The second was the adoption of the written word as a tool of education. Prior to that time, oral instruction prevailed and it was only with reluctance that writing was permitted to coexist with the spoken word in the classroom.

The third revolution came with the invention of printing and the subsequent wide availability of books.

The fourth revolution in Ashby's view is brought about by developments in electronics, notably those involving the radio, television, tape-recorder etc.

The implications of the fourth revolution in Ashby's view is "any technology which increases the rate of learning would enable the teacher to teach less and the learner to learn more."

## Development of Educational Technology — A Brief History

We may study the development of educational technology in three different groups of events as follows:

*I. 14th Century.* Instruction was restricted to mouth at the initial stage and then to manuscript. It is not that the teachers of this period failed to notice the importance of individual differences or motivation. But they put more emphasis on manuscript.

In the 15th century the art of printing was developed.

Books were printed. However, they were mostly on topics of religion and grammar.

In the 16th century, Peter Ramus introduced text-books in higher education.

*II. 17th Century.* In the second group, we peep into the 17th century and here we see John Comenius introducing text-books for children. He produced an illustrated book in 1657—"Orbus Pictures." He wrote about a hundred text-books. But the circulation was very much limited. J. Rosseau, H. Spencer, Froebel, Pesstallozi etc. helped in changing the concept of instruction and pupils. The child was put into the centre. Next came John Dewey. He tried to introduce the scientific method in education. E. Thorndike conducted experiments and put forward the learning theories. Then came John Adam's concrete-abstract continuum, i.e. define the object—show a model—diagram and then come to the verbal description.

*III. 20th Century.* In this century, we had other sciences like sound recording, photography etc. being developed and these added to the processor learning and teaching. Even electronic transmission was advancing. And all these aided the development of educational technology.

In this third group we enter into the era of First and Second World Wars. During the World War-I, the testing movement started. Binet was the forefather of this movement. During the World War-II, we could see the application of behavioural sciences to teaching and learning. In between, by 1925 Sidney L. experimented with programmed instruction. During 1938 and 1940, the concept of visual aids helped the process of learning. It thus paved the way for audio-visual education. In 1954 we got Edgar Dale's "Cone of Experience." Also during the same period, Weiner studied human engineering and also worked on the science of cybernetics.

By 1950, the world had also got Instructional Theories by Bruno, Glasser etc. In 1953; Gordan Pask applied the principles of cybernetics to education, in 1970, different developments took place and the concept of Educational Technology took its shape more neatly. Pioneering work in CAI (Computerised Applied Instruction) was carried out by Pask.

Development of communication, system-approach, social psychology (inter-group relationship), human factor approach to behavioural science—all these contributed to the development of educational technology. So also the audio-visual movements contributed to the development of education technology.

By this, it is clear how the things in the field of education changed their original shapes and formed into an altogether new one. But the question that now arose was: "Is audiovisual education different from the principles of educational technology?" The answer to this is as given on next page.

While thus going through the history of educational technology, it is also essential to note certain important events that helped for the development of educational technology. The Government of India sent a proposal to establish a centre for curriculum and media development under the United Nations Development and Programme Scheme (UNDP) and this proposal was approved in 1970 by Wilber Schramm. It was, therefore, felt by the Indian educationists to have a Centre for Educational Technology at Delhi and accordingly it was established at NCERT. Then in 1973, another unit for educational technology in the Ministry of Education was also established. After this the Government of India wanted educational technology cells to be established in different states. Today, we have educational technology cells in thirteen different states, among them being, Maharashtra, Gujarat, Orissa, Madhya Pradesh, Andhra Pradesh, Karnataka, Uttar

Pradesh, Rajasthan and Tamil Nadu. Educational Technology cells have also been started at all the four Regional Colleges of Education, that is, at Bhopal, Ajmer, Mysore and Bhubaneswar.

| Audio-Visual Aids | Educational Technology |
|---|---|
| 1. Audio-visual aids only try to improve the quality of the message. | 1. Educational technology concentrates on the psychological principles. |
| 2. Audio-visual aids ignore the individual differences. | 2. Educational technology emphasises on individual differences. |
| 3. Audio-visual aids do not take into consideration the enrichment of other fields. | 3. Educational technology' takes into consideration the development of social anthropology. |
| 4. Audio-visual aids are only materials | 4. Educational technology is definitely a technique. |

The problems posed by educational technology are:

(a) Will educational technology routinise education by using different methods?

(b) Will it kill the initiative of the teacher and the learner?

(c) Will it forward specialisation or will it go in for generalisation?

(d) Will it disintegrate the school system?

(e) Will it dehumanise education?

## Definition and Meaning of Educational Technology

It is needless to say that by now the reader's curiosity is roused enough to know what exactly is the definition of educational technology and what it means. Let us first peep through the varied definitions given by different people. However, in order to understand these definitions of educational technology, it is better to understand the terms "education," and 'technology" and then the term "educational technology".

*Education:* The word "education" has been derived from the Latin verb "educare" meaning "to train" to "instruct", "to put in" as also "to draw out" or to "lead forth". The word "education" has also teen understood as development of the power of adaptation to an ever-changing social environment.

*Technology:* It is a science of techniques and methods of doing or getting things done, related to any art, science or a particular profession. Technology has been defined as the science of "industrial arts"; and it is also defined as the application of science to the needs of an individual and the society. Technology is a scientific way of developing new techniques, and a systematic way of evolving and applying these techniques. Technology is thus a method of designing techniques.

*Educational Technology:* G.O.M. Leith (1975) defined "educational technology" as "an application of scientific knowledge about learning and the conditions of learning to improve the effectiveness and efficiency of teaching and training."

Thus it can be observed that educational technology has three important components:

(a) defining of educational goals in specific and clear terms;

(b) designing of instructional strategies and learning sequences; and

(c) evaluation of outcomes so as to obtain indicators of success or worth lessness of educational strategies.

John Leedham (1973) offered a definition of the term "educational technology" by giving a special consideration to the adaptive role of the teacher. According to him, "Educational technology concerns the systematic use of modem methods and technologies in teaching and learning. It involves teachers in a variety of roles, some of which are traditional, some still emerging."

He observed that during the development of programmed learning, closed circuit television and computer aided instruction, the role of the teachers, however varied, has been the critical one in determining the effectiveness of learning. One purpose of studying educational technology is surely to help us to make the best use of the capabilities of individual teachers and it seems unrealistic to accept any definition which does not specifically include the role of the teacher. There is agreement that earlier attempts to use teaching machines effectively failed because they were employed more as an alternative to the presence of a teacher than as an extension of his or her capabilities.

Some other definitions of educational technology are as follows:

(a) The International Commission on the Development of Education defined "educational technology" as follows: "Educational technology means the intellectual and operational efforts to rearrange, to regroup or to systematise application of scientific methods for the organisation of (scientific method) equipment and material to optimise the learning process."

(b) The definition given by the National Council for Educational Technology says: "Educational technology means the development, application and evaluation of three different things: (i) techniques; (ii) systems and (iii) aids to improve the process of human learning".

(c) According to UNESCO specialists, "Educational Technology is a communication process resulting from application of scientific methods to the behavioural science of teaching and learning: This communication process may or may not require the use of a media such as radio film, television broadcasts, cassettes etc.

The main components of this communication process are:

— goals of behavioural objectives,
— analysis of the characteristics of learners,
— selection and organisation of content,
— selection of media,
— evaluation, and
— feedback.

(d) According to Dr. B.P. Lulla, "Educational technology is the application of scientific methods and techniques to education."

(e) To quote Derik Unwin, "educational technology is concerned with the application of modern skills and techniques to the requirements of education and training."

(f) Robert Glasser describes the process of educational technology in the following components:

— different students learn in different ways and at different rates;
— different kinds of skills, abilities, knowledge and understanding are required in different ways;
— the various elements of instruction themselves have different learning characteristics;
— the elements in the learning process should not be considered apart from each other as each has some bearing on education;
— as far as possible, any learning system should be self-correcting which means that it should have

some built-in arrangement of evaluation and feedback which can be used to improve it.

Thus educational technology in the widest sense implies a behavioural science approach to teaching and learning in that it makes use of pertinent scientific and technological methods and concepts developed in psychology, sociology, communication, linguistics and other related fields.

To make the discussion more clear, it is better to know what answer Collier (1977) has given to the question: "What is educational technology?" Collier quotes a recent book on Educational Technology thus: "This book is not about audio-visual aids. My aim is not to promote television. Educational technology is not to be confused with electronic gadgetry. Educational technology is as wide as education itself; it is concerned with the design and evaluation of curriculum and learning experiences and with the problem of implementing and renovating them. Essentially, it is a rational problem solving approach to education, a way of thinking skeptically and systematically about learning and teaching."

The above description also gives a vivid picture of what educational technology is and what is not. The dictionary meaning of the term "technology" includes the application of knowledge for practical ends, a branch of knowledge that deals with industrial arts, applied science, engineering etc., the use of machines to eliminate manual labour, for improving human productivity etc. The Council of Educational Technology of Britain has given a comprehensive definition of this term thus: "The development, application and evaluation of systems, techniques and aids to improve the process of human learning."

Educational technology can be considered as the systematic use of scientific methods to plan, realise and evaluate effective teaching and learning process in informal and non-formal situations. Educational technology as it exists today is comparatively a new idea; grown as a result of the integration of technological devices in the use of practices with the newly explored psychological principles of learning, teaching, behavioural modification, content analysis, education etc.

In the use of educational technology, the publishing industry has adopted terms like "software" and "hardware." "Software" are the tangible stimulus items such as educational films, slides, programmed materials, etc.; whereas the mechanical instruments needed for the projection or display of the software, such as film projectors, slide projectors, teaching machines etc. are known as hardware. Both hardware and software are needed in the use of educational technology. Although hardward are a necessary component of educational technology, they by themselves remain of little use unless the concomitant component of a suitable software is fed with it. Thus a technology of instruction is concerned with a few tools and techniques which can be used to make the teaching and learning process more effective. It is an integration of software and hardware.

Educational technology includes a wider range of hardware, starting from the chalkboard and the boards for charts, pictorial illustrations, printed materials etc. up to advanced mass media such as computer and communication satellites.

However, it is still essential to look deeply into the hardware aspect of educational technology: ET-1 and also the software aspect of Educational technology: ET-2.

**Hardware Aspect: ET-1**

The hardware approach is also called High Technology, and is based on the application of engineering principles for developing electro-chemical equipments like motion pictures, tape-recorders, teaching machines, computers, video-tapes, closed circuit television, etc. Their approach to educational technology is a by-product of the scientific and technological developments. Davies (1971) thinks that the hardware approach is based on the application of physical sciences to the education and training system, which mechanises the process of teaching gradually so that teachers would be able to deal with more students resulting in loss cost and economy in educational finances. Thus, the process of teaching/learning has been gradually mechanised through the use of teaching machines, radio, language laboratory, tape-recorders, video-tapes and projectors.

**Software Aspect: ET-2**

The software aspect of educational technology is also known as Low Technology. This refers to technology in a generic sense. Any material which is made reproducible and whose quality and output are controlled can be classified under ET-2. All programmed learning materials come under ET-2.

ET-2 uses the principles of psychology for behaviour modification purposes. It esteems the pioneer effects of Skinner and also other behaviourists for the development of ET-2. It is the application of scientific knowledge in learning, and conditions of learning to improve the effectiveness and efficiency of learning and training. The techniques of programmed learning employes the findings of the science of learning to classroom instruction. It refers to the application of teaching/learning principles to the direct and deliberate shaping of behaviour. Its origin lies in the application of behaviour science.

These two meanings of educational technology—the first, concerned with teaching aids like teaching machines, and the second, with learning aids like programmed instruction are functionally related to each other.

## Trends in Educational Technology

The two major trends that have developed in the process of educational technology are: (1) technology for mass instruction and (ii) technology for individual instruction. Included in the first type are instructional broadcasting, television filmed lectures, CCTV, motion pictures etc. Under technology for individual instruction, there are equipments and materials designed for individual operation such as teaching machines, programmed instruction, auto-tutorial system, computer-assisted instruction, language laboratories, learning modules etc.

## Programmed Instruction

In a fast developing world, the teacher cannot and ought not to be left alone to depend upon his own resources and talents to disseminate knowledge to the pupils. The classroom teacher should be supplied with reliable instructional material based upon the dependable findings of educational technology. This will help him to do his job with maximum perfection. Programmed learning is one such big steps in this direction. In this the subject-mater or content of the course displays a few distinct characteristics such as:

(i) a clear-cut statement of the objectives;

(ii) the material to be learned is itemised and presented serially;

(iii) frequent and unambiguous responses from every student are required throughout the whole sequence. Unless the learner makes some responses which are relevant to the learning task, no learning will occur;

(iv) feedback of information about the correctness or otherwise of the responses is given to the pupil before the next frame or item is presented.

## Modular Scheduling

A module is a short unit of instruction dealing with a single conceptual unit of subject matter. Each course is built in the "bank" of a number of modules and each module is designed around a list of objectives and student projects. A variety of learning activities centred around the learner and incorporating a multi-media approach is provided. The components of modules include modular lecture unit, laboratory unit, programmed instruction unit, workshop unit, individual study unit, film unit, audio-tape unit, video-tape unit etc.

## Multi-media Approach

For effective and efficient learning, it is now accepted that there should be a multi-media approach. Edgar Dale (1969) through his "Cone of Experience" has demonstrated that in any learning situation, the more the senses are stimulated, the more the person learns and the longer he retains. Dale describes how the different types of aids, starting from verbal symbols up to direct purposeful experiences, are interrelated and effective in the learning process. The different materials of the experiences presented in the cone may be classified into three: (1) non-projected aids; (ii) projected aids; and (iii) activity aids.

The following are some specific applications of instructional technology in imparting formal education:

1. Use films, television, slide-tape presentation and so forth as an alternative to a lecture for presentation of information.
2. Buy, borrow or produce 2″ ×2″ colour slides, showing the steps in a process to be demonstrated.
3. Use an opaque projection to show a printed diagramme.

4. Make a transparency from a cartoon or drawing in a few seconds on a thermographic copier and show it to the class using an overhead projector (OHP).
5. Draw chalkboard diagrams once on transparency master; then project the transparencies made from these masters on OHP, thus saving the time wasted in rewording them each year.
6. Record questions, problems, exercises and background information on different subjects or at different levels of difficulty on tape for use by individuals or small groups with cassette play-back units. While some students are interacting with the recorded material, you will be free to work intensively with the others.

## Meaning of "Educational Technology"

Words are of little interest in themselves but they do indicate changes in thinking. Once the climate of opinion is right, one may arrive at the word Educational Technology" by different routes. One route starts from audio-visual aids! At first sight, it would appear that teaching machines could go under this heading; but those who work with teaching machines emphasise the importance of programmes rather than machinery. Hence the heading has to become audio-visual aids and programmed instruction, an odd pairing since some forms of programmed instructions use only the printed

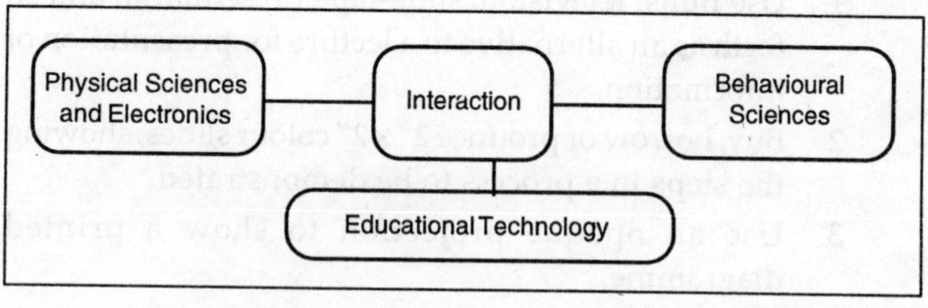

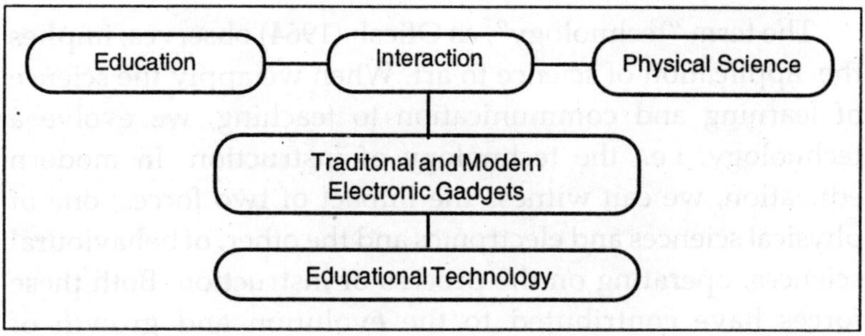


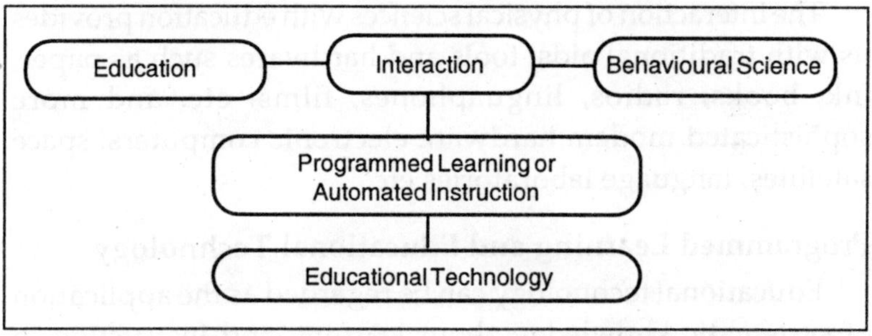


page. The new term "educational technology" suggests itself and it may be used to refer to a little beyond the use of equipments and techniques that are associated with equipments. On the other route, starting from programmed instruction, a wider conception of educational technology tends to be reached. It is difficult to keep programmed instruction within narrow bounds. Programmed instruction begins to look as though it is a part of something larger and this is educational or instructional technology. Programmed instruction emphasises that the aims of teaching should be analysed, the methods of accomplishing them made explicit and 'he effects assessed as precisely as possible. These basic ideas are applicable to the systems of instruction that do not necessarily include the use of teaching machines.

The term "technology", as Ofiesh (1964) observes, implies the application of science to art. When we apply the science of learning and communication to teaching, we evolve a technology, i.e., the technology of instruction. In modern education, we can witness the impact of two forces; one of physical sciences and electronics and the other, of behavioural sciences, operating on the process of instruction. Both these forces have contributed to the evolution and growth of educational technology. Fig. 2 makes the concept clear.

The interaction of physical sciences with education provides us with traditional aids, tools and hardwares such as paper, ink, books, radios, linguaphones, films, etc. and more sophisticated modem hardware electronic computers, space satellites, language laboratories etc.

**Programmed Learning and Educational Technology**

Educational technology can be regarded as the application of systematic knowledge about learning and instruction to teaching and training with the aim of improving their quality and efficiency. For this reason, a wide range of presentation, control and feedback devices may be employed such as teaching machines, stimulators and computers. It should, however be emphasised that techniques such as critical path analysis, curriculum development methods and task analysis are essential components as well as the hardware system. In fact, as long as programmed learning coordinates these techniques, it is woven into the fabric of educational technology.

The point is that it is not merely a system of presentation, a particular technique or a set of principles; it is a methodology for discovering an efficient means of organising learning situations to attain specified objectives.

Looked at from another point of view, the job of the programmer can be regarded as that of providing appropriate opportunities for the pupils to learn. It is his task to discover what these may be and to arrange the environment of learning, as far as he is able to optimise these opportunities. He will, for example, have to determine in some cases whether simulation is as useful as the real thing in some learning situations.

Programmed learning, though wide in scope, is only a part of the broader concept of educational technology which must include many areas such as the problem of innovation, resources of learning, standardisation and compatibility of system components, the training of personnel, educational productivity and the design of educational plant.

If educational technology possesses any value at all, it is vital that the teachers in training shall be introduced to its philosophy and techniques.

In fact, there are two meanings attached to the definition of the term "educational technology." One meaning refers to the detailed application of psychology of learning to practical teaching problems. The second meaning refers to the application of engineering principles in the development of electro-mechanical equipments of such devices—pictures, tape-recorders, computers etc.

These two meanings of educational technology interact in the design and use of equipment to provide control over the learning situation, a rich array of stimulus materials (e.g., films) and interaction between responses of the learner and the presentation of instructional material.

However, the correct meaning of the term "educational technology' has been differentiated by Lumsdaine by using two different symbols: ET-1, ET-2. 'ET-1' refers to the application of technology to instrumentation useful to the process of leaching. This meaning in its essence is a hardware approach. It stresses the need to develop and use audio-visual aids for teaching. Due to this concept, the process of teaching is mechanised through production and use of leaching aids.

ET-2 means the application of scientific principles to instruction and hence the emphasis is on objectives and performances. It is the software aspect. All programmed learning materials and leaching machines dime under this.

Educational technology is thus the application of scientific knowledge about learning and conditions of learning to improve she effectiveness of teaching and learning.

**Nature of Educational Technology**

So far no one is universally agreed upon the, definition of the term educational technology." For most people the term brings to mind such electronic gadgetry as film projectors, tape recorders, television sets and micro-computers used as leaching tools. Other people add such non-electrical instructional materials as books, photographs and charts. Still others subscribe to a definition that includes not only items used in teaching but also equipments used in educational administration—keeping students' records on the micro film, communicating between schools by radio, correcting entrance examination papers with the aid of a computer and the like.

In effect, educational technology can mean different things to different people. Even those who have specialised in this field have failed to arrive at a proper definition. However, in an attempt to satisfy everyone, the Association for Educational Communications and Technology in the United States have come to the following definition: "Educational technology is a complex integrated process involving people, procedures, ideas, devices and organisation for analysing problems and devising, implementing, evaluating and managing solutions to those problems involved in all aspects of learning."

Extensive use of educational technology requires a lot of

change on the part of the teacher. This is because some technologies are not accepted or only partly accepted because they require too many adjustments of traditional methods of instruction or administration. Frequently, teachers avoid attempting a new instructional technique because it requires too much from them in energy, time, patience or skill to become adept in its use. Altering old leaching habits in order to master new ones entails not only the expenditure of energy but also the risk of a toucher looking foolish by committing embarrassing errors when attempting new techniques in she classroom. In addition, touchers who have traditionally perceived themselves as classroom's chief performers — lecturing, conducting recitations, leading class discussion — can feel demoted to a less prestigious educational role when they are asked to have reading materials, radio, television or computers to deliver the content of lessons.

Thus the amount of change required in the existing habits and the fear of failure or of decreased prestige can affect the teachers' willingness to accept a new technology. Electronic equipment may frighten teachers with its apparent complexity. At least a part of this fear comes from the expectation that something may go wrong during the lesson, making the teacher appear inept or unable to control the teaching situation. To utilise educational television (ETV), many teachers think that much training equipment and general reevaluation of teaching goals and activities would be required. However, such fears are baseless.

The evolution of technology has in fact ushered in a kind of revolution in or occupational, social and educational world. But it seems a little awkward to observe that whereas the contribution of some kind of technology is visibly felt in respect of the operation of our hospitals, factories, farms and offices, our classrooms have remained a unique example of backwardness by remaining insensitive to the technological inputs and their influences. The reasons for this are not far to seek. Our teacher and via him/her the processes of educational resource generation have not properly assimilated or understood the importance and relevance of technology for the classroom. Also the overall ecology of the formal educational system is responsible to a considerable extent for this state of affairs.

Earlier educators used to advocate the use of audio-visual aids in the process of teaching in addition to supplementary aids such as pictures, charts, maps, models and various audio-aids. Gradually, the emphasis shifted to the employment of costly gadgets such as video and computers and now the multi-media approach.

In brief, it may then be said that the entire principle of educational technology lies in the:

(1) Use of a broad range of resources:
(2) Emphasis on individualised learning; and
(3) Emphasis on systems approach to education.

**Aims of Educational Technology**

Educational technology aims at facilitating and improving human learning. However, the following two are the important aims:

(1) To provide appropriately designed situations for learning and teaching, i.e., those situations which keep in mind the objectives that are necessary for training.
(2) To modify the learner's environment by presentation of material, by arranging the different learning activities and by organising the physical and social surroundings of the learner.

## Functions of Educational Technology

In a nutshell, it may be stated that educational technology has specified goals and also it has definite behavioural objectives. Further, it analyses the characteristics of learners. Next it is concerned with the selection and organisation of content/subject matter to be learned. Educational technology is also concerned with the presentation of the content and most importantly it is helpful in the evaluation of results (computers).

On account of these facts, feedback no more remains a final component but provides an essential linkage between all the components. It is concerned with the designed learning situations.

## Need of Educational Technology

George Kneller (1961) comments that "Education must mirror the age it strives to improve. It can not isolate itself from isolation any more than from other social or economic changes."

Finn (1968) argues that in a technologically-oriented society, education should wed itself to science and technology. Education cannot wall itself off from the technological advances.

Stolurow (1963) argues that three major factors demand the adaptation of technology to education. These are:

(a) The exploding world population;
(b) The exponential rate at which new knowledge is being generated;
(c) The changing science and technology of our current society.

In the Indian context, the following factors further prompt education to court technology:

(a) Problems of education like free primary education and eradication of adult illiteracy can never be solved through conventional teaching techniques.

(b) The deterioration of falling standards can be checked and quality instruction can be imparted, if educational technology and programmed learning material are yoked to conventional classroom teaching.

(c) There are millions and millions of learners who cannot afford to join schools and colleges for continuing their formal education. Through educational technology, we can give them the best possible instruction while they stay at home.

(d) The much difficult task of teaching foreign or other regional languages can be quickly accomplished if educational technology is utilised in the service of language learning.

(e) For transmitting better ideas and developing accurate thinking, technological aids are the only means. They impart the fast increasing knowledge in various disciplines in a short period with best retention.

(f) Ours is a country of unique geographic vastness, racial diversity and inhabited by people of different cultures, languages, traditions an customs, in which educational technology plays a unique role in developing national integration.

(g) India being one of the biggest democracies of the world, it is of paramount importance to educate the pubic about universal franchise, fundamental rights and responsibility which can only be possible with the help of modern electronic gadgets—radio, television and space satellite (Ex: SITE Programme).

(h) Most of our population lives in villages. They are mostly illiterate, superstitious and occasionally fall a prey to the deadly diseases and epidemics, who can be educated about the rampant social evils such as exploitation of man by man, the caste system, social and economic discrimination, untouchability etc. only through educational technology.

(i) The main occupation of the people in the villages is agriculture, so our farmers can be equipped with the vital knowledge abut the latest methods of crop rearing, the use of better and improved seeds, use of fertilisers and pesticides etc. only with the help of educational technology.

**Scope of Educational Technology**

By taking into consideration the usefulness of educational technology in all branches of education, one dare not deny the vastness of its scope. It modifies the learner's environment through the various techniques of presentation, arrangement of learning activities and organisation of physical surroundings.

The very purpose of educational technology is to facilitate and improve the quality of human learning. It is concerned with achieving the goals—of maintaining internal discipline, adapting to its environment etc. For solving the varied problems of education successfully, educational technology consisting of various media of mass communication, suitable child learning processes, and modern testing and evaluation techniques are essential. Especially in developing countries like India, it has to be mastered and utilised by educationists if they are to keep pace with each other and catch up with the developed nations. As such bot quantitative expansion and qualitative improvement of education can be facilitated and accelerated with the help of educational technology.

Today, technology of education is being developed with the aim not only of making education more widely available, but also of improving the quality of education which is already available.

Education technology is conceptualised audio-visual aids. What can it achieve most? Only to improve the quality of message and if it is taken in the form of problem-oriented techniques, then its main concern will be the production of teaching-learning material. But both these meanings make the scope limited because educational technology is also concerned with the management and organisation of man and material both, so that they achieve the specific objectives of planing and implementation.

Educational technology is concerned with providing appropriately designed learning situations, which hold in view the objectives of teaching. In modifies the learner's environment through the varied techniques of presentation, arrangement of learning activities and organisation and physical surroundings. The purpose of educational technology prove the quality of human learning.

The uniqueness of educational technology is characterised as

1. Use of a broad range of resources for learning;
2. Emphasis on individualised learning; and
3. Use of systems approach.

The effectiveness of educational technology depends on:

1. Ability to achieve goals;
2. To maintain itself internally; and
3. To adapts to its environment.

Educational technology is concerned with the disciplined and systematic approach to education and training. It is a sort of investment in national development. Employment structures can be neatly geared to make the best need of development. Employment structures can be neatly geared to make the best need of development. The entire educational system is educational technology adapting itself to the changing environmental conditions. Thus the scope of educational technology has become very vast.

Technology includes:

1. Preparing pupils for learning experiences:
2. Reinforcing their values while pupils are sharing the experience;
3. Relating the experience with the lesson and thus stimulating further learning.

However, the factors responsible for the progress of educational technology also cannot be overlooked. The factors causing the progress of educational technology are:

1. Student flood due to population explosion;
2. Acute resources scarcities;
3. Rising costs;
4. Unsuitability of output.

Hence there must be a focus on relationships of things between the various levels and internal working parts between the educational system and the environmental.

There is a heavy stress on innovation to achieve the needed improvements and adjustments. This requires modernisation in educational management, modernisation of teachers, of learning process, strengthening of educational finance and emphasis on non-formal education.

If educational technology will not cater to individualised learning, then there will be no individual development and social progress.

Taking education as a life-long process, individuals learn from their life experiences and this can be achieved only through educational technology—by carrying out individual activities like library work, group projects games, instructions with aids and also through programmed learning.

**Limitation of Educational Technology**

(1) Non-availability of the services of well-learned and well-educated personnel in rural schools.

(2) Unsystematic use of varied methodologies in rural schools. Educational technology brings together the psychology of learning behaviour as well as the communication system. But in underdeveloped areas, this cannot be fully achieved. The use of learning systems such as programmed learning has become a challenge today and this challenge is definitely met by educational technology by its varied techniques.

In fact, the scope of educational technology depends upon the context in which the term "educational technology" is used. In the first case, if the term is used in terms of audio-visual aids, mechanical and electrical gadgets, the scope is limited to improving the educational messages. But if the term is used as process-oriented technique, then its scope is limited to the production of teaching-learning material. The rigorous task analysis specification of direct behaviour, the determination of pre-requisites and the gradual development of the programme ensures that the teaching-learning material developed in this style will be most useful to the learner. Thus, in this sense, educational technology is basically a technique of developing software. Hence the correct step consists of outlining the educational problem by rigorously thinking about the following aspects:

(1) Availability of resources at home;

(2) Resources that am re managed by external assistance;

(3) Clear specification of the problem;

(4) The constraints that hinder the probable situation;

(5) How different resources interact with one another.

It is true to say that the scope of educational technology ranges from the most concrete to the most abstract and subtle ones. In almost all the important activities engaged in the name of teaching-training or instruction, the possibility of using educational technology has already been explored in the past and is being explored even today.

Rowntree (1973) says that educational technology is Identifying aims and objectives, planning and learning environment, exploring and structuring the subject matter, selecting the appropriate teaching strategies and learning media, evaluating the worthwhileness of learning systems and using the insights gained from evaluation to improve the effectiveness for the future. These are specific concerns and hence the province educational technology.

## Summing Up

The term "educational technology" is interpreted in two distinct ways:

(1) to describe the use of technology in education; or

(2) to imply the concept of technology of education.

The former is concerned with the use of equipment and the latter with improving the effectiveness of learning. The concept of educational technology implies a systematic approach to learning in which one tries to develop means to achieve the given ends and persists in one's attempts to find solutions to problems. Although, in a narrow way, educational technology means a little more than the use of sophisticated hardware in teaching like overhead projectors, televised films, cassettes, videos, gramophones etc., in a broad way it may be interpreted to mean the use of any new technique or method of teaching. Technology of education would include the entire process of setting goals, the continuous renewal of curriculum, the trying out and use of new methods and materials in view of changing circumstances. It is often identified with the various devices and means of recording, storage, manipulation, retrieval, transmission and display of data and information with high efficiency and at great speed. They are considered as an integral part of a broad curriculum for research and development design amounting to tremendous potentialities in education. Technological media and materials useful in the instructional process range from simple varieties of aid to teachers to develop and present his/her lessons more effectively in the traditional classroom to sophisticated machines and mechanisms completely changing the classroom teaching structure and situation.

Educational technology is useful in making learning experiences practical and therefore, better related to life's goals, it has peeped into the fields of motivation, sensation-perception, attention, evaluation etc. Educational technology can be used effectively for formal, informal, non-formal systems of education of whatever level it may be.

The growing use of educational technology in today's schools has helped to release the learner from the routine role of "information giving," so that he/she can devote his/her time and effort to the more important asks of planning, arranging and evaluating learning experiences and outcomes and to encourage, guide, counsel pupils. The various technological media are used to communicate the needed factual information to pupils and they are capable of doing this perhaps more accurately and efficiently than the teacher.

# 5

# Transfer of Training

There was prevalent among the educators a doctrine namely "Mental Discipline," during the latter half of the 19th century. This doctrine, mind consisted of faculties such as memory, will, reasoning, imagination and so on. These faculties were likened to muscles that could be trained or strengthed by appropriate exercises. It was a kind of mental gymnastics. This represented the Faculty School of psychology. Subjects such as Philosophy, Latin, Greek, mathematics, literature were the choicest materials for rigorous training and sharpening of these faculties. Hence it was called Formal Discipline. This theory was defended by its protagonists on the grounds that the products of this kind of curriculum turned out to be most cultured and sophisticated in consequence. In yore days, education was accessible only to the privileged minority in society. Only those gifted with extraordinary ability pursued formal education. These people were intelligent by nature. It is not as though the curriculum made them intelligent. They were intelligent enough to profit from a tough curriculum comprising classical languages, Mathematics, Logic etc., etc. They were under the mistaken notion that a tough curriculum could discipline the minds of students. One who has mastered Greek and Latin would have developed his Memory and will-power so well that he could use it in many other areas of learning. Similarly, Mathematics and Logic would have sharpened their reasoning power to such an extent that it could be used in any other field as well.

### *Positive, Negative and Zero Transfer*

When learning in one activity "facilitates" learning in a new or similar task positive transfer occurs. For example, a student's learning of arithmetic may be positively transferred when he takes up Accounting at a later stage.

Negative transfer takes place when learning in one area "interferes" with or "blocks" learning in another area. For example parents who had learnt Biology in the old, traditional way invariably experience difficulty with their children's "New Biology" book. Learning the rules of driving on the right hand side of the road in the Europe presents trouble for the sight-seeing American tourist who rents a car in a country like Pakistan where driving is on the left side of the road.

Positive transfer occurs in a variety of situations. As a consequence of learning to spell the word "house," a child may be able to apply the appropriate' phonetic rule and correctly spell the word "mouse". At the same time a child's experience in learning the plural of 'house' (i.e. houses) may be detrimental to his learning the plural of "mouse (which is mice)."

### *Principle of Transfer*

When the responses expected from two tasks or learning situations are similar positive transfer takes place. When the tasks require the same or similar response to a stimulus, even if the stimuli in the two situations are different positive transfer occurs. The positive transfer effects become stronger and stronger when the similarity between the responses called for in the previous learning and new learning becomes more and more. However, the maximum amount of positive transfer is obtained when the stimulus and response elements in the previous learning and the new learning situations are similar. e.g. Learning of 9 × 5 = 45 would greatly facilitate learning of 5 × 9 = 45. Maximum positive transfer takes place when the stimuli and response in the two tasks are identical mostly.

Negative transfer occurs when stimuli require different responses. For instance one may learn to pronounce the word 'read' as it is expressed in the sentence, "Ask Hari to read the book." Having learned the pronunciation of the word 'read' as used in the above example, he may try to pronounce it is the same manner while reading a sentence, "Has Hari read the book?" In both cases the stimulus word is the same, but the responses required in the two are different. In this first case the word is pronounced as 'read' whereas in the second case it should be pronounced as 'red.'

When the stimuli and responses in the previous and the new learning situations are dissimilar or completely different little or no transfer occurs. For instance, learning to add numbers probably may not have any direct effect on the learning to spell words. Learning 15 + 15 = 30 may not facilitate, or hinder learning to spell the word 'Deer.' However, the general methods of work and rules involved in learning two tasks, even if the stimuli and responses are different, may be carried over from one situation to another facilitating positive transfer. This happens mainly due to the *Learning to Learn* phenomenon.

*(i) Judd's Theory of Generalised Principles*

According to this theory the process of transfer is based on an understanding of the principle or "Generalisation" underlying the responses made in two or more activities. If a general principle is understood all the example of the principle will be put into perspective and readily understood.

*(i) Thorndike's Theory of Identical Elements*

According to this theory each activity is composed of many precise movements and connections. Transfer occurs to the extent the two activities share certain elements. The amount of transfer is proportional to the number of identical elements or components in the two learning situations. The term "components" suggested by Woodworth refers to complex factors whereas 'elements' is atomic. The amount of transfer depends on the degree to which they both involve responses using the same concepts, operations and symbols. e.g. Study of Biology helps one in the study of Medicine and study of Mathematics helps in the study of Engineering and Technology.

*(iii) Bagley's Transfer of Attitudes Theory*

Common attitudes, ideals and ego-involvement constituted factors of transfer according to Bagley. Particularly for transfer of traits like honesty, neatness etc., common attitudes to the two fields are necessary. Otherwise, one may be honest at home and dishonest at school. Bagley has emphasised that such qualities should be taught and accepted in ideals so that the "ego" of the person would be involved.

*(iv) Intelligence and Transfer*

The higher the IQ (Intelligence Quotient) the more capable one is of positive transfer. Spearman tells transfer involving the General or "G" factor of intelligence. The ability to perceive relations, reorganise experiences and adapt one's responses to new situations are all functions of the "G" factor.

*(v) Gestalt' Transposability of Insight*

The Gestalt psychologists view transfer as the consequence of "transposability of Insight". Transposition theories have also been called as patterns of experience. This theory for the first time was developed by Max Wertheimer. A 'Gestalt' is a whole, the behaviour of which is not determined by that of its individual element but when the part processes are themselves determined by the intrinsic nature of the whole.

*(vi) Motivation and Transfer*

Transfer does not take place automatically. This "intent" to learn and the "will" to achieve helps a great deal in transfer. Naturally, it engages a known effort on the part of the teacher to plan learning experiences that will encourage learners "to look for" and "exploit" situations that lead to transfer. More of illustrations can be of great help in this regard.

*(vi) Bilateral Transfer*

Bilateral transfer (cross education) from one limb to another is evident. Learning a skill with one's right hand facilitates its acquisition later through the left hand.

(a) Identify instructional goals and formulate in specific behavioural terms.
(b) Organise the material in a proper order of difficulty such that the easier parts are learnt before the difficult aspects are faced.
(c) Give a variety of examples taken from mundane life and encourage students to cite examples.
(d) Encourage an attitude of open-mindedness.
(e) Teach techniques of problem-solving and methods of inquiry.
(f) Teach students the method of "learning to learn...."
(g) Use guided discussion and class projects.
(h) Ignite imagination of students to learn more beyond what has been taught in the classroom.

## QUESTIONS

1. How do you explain 'Bilateral Transfer'?
2. What does Thorndike mean by "identical elements."?

3. What is the relation between motivation and transfer?
4. Define transfer of training.
5. What is the relation between IQ and transfer.
6. Describe the historical roots of transfer.
7. What should be the guiding principles in curriculum framing?
8. Enumerate the principles behind stimulus—response relationship and the kind of transfer.
9. Describe Judd's experiment on generalisation.
10. What is 'mental gymnastics'?

# 6

# Educational Technology Frontiers

Of late, 'Educational Technology' has advanced by leaps and bounds. May it be the hardware or the software aspect, theory or its application, system or component, there is an alround progress. Research, innovations and developments on the frontiers of educational technology are leading us to new heights. Researches on the applications of new technologies enable us to adopt the more promising and shed off the unfavourable ones. In this module, we look at some of the latest aspects of educational technology.

**Prerequisites**

It is only fair that the learner should be aware of the past and present of educational technology before sharing thoughts on the futuristic aspects of the same. You are, therefore, well advised to go through the other modules before going through this one.

**Modular Objectives**

The objective of this module is that, on completion, you will be able to

— state some of the frontier areas of educational technology
— describe the plus points of interactive video

— outline different types of teleconferencing
— explain the need for focus on software development.

You may like to check how aware you already are as regards some of new developments in educational technology. Over 80% score means you are 'well-informed'!

| | Questions for Self-Assessment | | | Max. Points | Points Scored |
|---|---|---|---|---|---|
| 1. | State two frontiers in educational technology? | | | 2 | |
| | (a) | (b) | | | |
| 2. | State two recent modes of computer based education | | | 2 | |
| | (a) | (b) | | | |
| 3. | What are the main components of an interactive video system? | | | 3 | |
| | (a) | (b) | (c) | | |
| 4. | What is the storage capacity of a videodisc | | | 2 | |
| | ____________________ | | | | |
| 5. | List three plus points of videodisc over video cassette system | | | 3 | |
| | (a) | (b) | (c) | | |
| 6. | Differentiate between video-conferencing and audio-plus conferencing | | | 2 | |
| | ____________________ | | | | |
| 7. | Tabulate the relative merits of audio, computer and video conferencing | | | 3 | |
| | Audio | Computer | Video | | |
| 8. | What are the features of the latest software? | | | 3 | |
| | (a) | (b) | (c) | | |
| | | | Total | 20 | |
| | | | Your % Score | | |

## Where are the Frontiers?

Frontiers of research are in the beholder's eye. It is possible to research on the effectiveness of the chalkboard as also on the combined use of computer and video. Yes, chalkboard has been the focus of research all along. How else would you explain the innovations of magnetic chalk-board for magnet-backed cutouts, whiteboard for writing with dry-wipe colour markers, greyboard for video-recording, bulletin board for electronic display and electronic-photocopying chalkboards which provides a paper photocopy of the chalkwork on the press of a button!

Computer and video have a great reason to work together. All said and done in the previous modules, computer and video, taken individually, have serious limitations as far as instruction is concerned. More so, they are complimentary, i.e., plus points of the computer negate the negative points of video and plus points of video negate the negative points of the computer. Synthesis of the two have indeed resulted in a potential frontier in educational technology. This is variously called Computer Based Multimedia, Interactive Video or simply Multimedia. We shall refer to it as Interactive Video-Teleconferencing is another emerging area of great interest for distance-communication through audio, video or computers and through a combination of two or more of them. Interactions in real-time between two or more persons at long distances has opened up new vistas in distance education, group dynamics, problem solving and general communication. Videotex system and Facsimile transmission (FAX) have revolutionised the distant display and transmission of writing on documents.

Advances in software are both necessary and desirable in order to harness the potential of computer, video and other hardware systems. Authoring systems, knowledge-base systems with artificial intelligence and software for fifth-generation computers must be conceived and researched for learning effectiveness. In any case, there is an urgent need for the faculty members to research on their teaching methodologies, use of audiovisuals, evaluation techniques and so on. It is not merely the spot-learning of the students that constitutes the end goal; it is the development of study-skills, thinking skills, independent study habits and hence learning to learn which should also be in focus. How long will the researchers in educational psychology, teaching methodology and instructional technology have to research on pedagogy in other disciplines, say, science and engineering? Why I can't the faculty members take up the task of researching in pedagogy in their own disciplines? That is where the frontiers are.

**Interactive Video**

Computer-Based Instruction refers to instruction with the use of computers taking up one role or the other. Computers may aid or assist instruction, i.e., assist teaching, or learning or both. Computers may manage the learning activity by assuming the role of manager of learning. Computers may as well evaluate the learning outcome of a learner by maintaining a question bank, set a question paper by objectives, score the response of the candidates and finally process the results in a comprehensive manner. The above modes of instruction are termed as CBI, CAI, CAL, CAT, CMI and CAE respectively as schematised below.

**Computers in Education**

| | | |
|---|---|---|
| | | Learning |
| | Assisted | |
| COMPUTER | Aided | Instruction |
| | Based | Teaching |
| | Managed | Evaluation |

A newly coined term, computer-mediated learning CML, perhaps means one or more of the above. In addition, it may also include the Computer Based Multimedia, i.e.. Interactive Video. Another term gaining popularity is V-CAL which means Video-based Computer Assisted Learning.

Interactive video refers to computer assisted learning with video used in an interactive manner. Interactivity implies two-way communication. Attempts to provide interactivity with video by built-in questions / answers, by frequent pauses provided by the teacher and by way of group discussions in the trigger-video mode of teaching have sparked off the thought that computer-controlled video should create meaningful learning. Without computer, video is a passive medium; the computer can activate it.

Levels of interactivity on laservision, i.e., reflective optical laser-operated video disc defined by the Nebraska research group are now universally accepted. According to the Nebraska scale, the levels are 0, the lowest, 1, 2, 3, and 4, the highest imaginable.

**Levels of Interactivity**

| | |
|---|---|
| Level 0 | The bottom of the scale designed by the Nebraska Videodisc Design/Production Group to describe interactivity in videodisc players. Level 0 represents earlier domestic-standard players which have no potential for interactivity. |
| Level 1 | The first practical level of the Nebraska scale. Level 1 represents the basic features expected even on domestic equipment remote control, the 'search' facility, freeze frame, forward and reverse motion, and quick scan, slow motion and step frame replay. |
| Level 2 | The mid-point on the Nebraska scale. Level 2 player is one which, using only its own onboard microprocessor, can offer multiple choice, the branching facility and score-keeping. |
| Level 3 | Effectively the top of the Nebraska scale. Level 3 represents a video player, industrial or domestic, linked to an external computer (mainframe, mini or micro). Level 3 offers by far the greatest versatility of any interactive configuration. |
| Level 4 | In a practical interpretation, a complete workstation comprising video and computer equipment and furniture. Speculatively, the peak of the Nebraska scale. Level 4 still represents conjecture into the future of interactive technology, rather than actual applications, and can create merely hypothetical images; video can add real-life |

*contd...*

events and effects. Potential of video-computer link up appears to overcome all the limitations of either of them taken singly. The two together are electronically and pedagogically compatible. In interactive video, the student interacts with the computer and the computer, in turn, interacts with the video, calling video images wherever necessary. The student is thus provided with a variety of rich and meaningful learning experiences which neither video nor computer, nor teacher alone could create.

Man is developing multimedia in his own reflection. Human beings are perhaps the most versatile multimedia. Let us look at a comparison of the two.

**Multimedia vis-a-vis Human Being**

| Human Capabilities | Multimedia Capabilities |
|---|---|
| A human being can: | Multimedia can: |
| * write | * print |
| * draw lines | * draw lines |
| * make graphics | * make graphics |
| * draft pictures | * show pictures |
| * talk | * play voice |
| * sing | * play music |
| * respond to touch | * respond to touch-screen, Kyboard, mouse, etc. |
| * see and react | * respond to hand movement |
| * respond to voice | * respond to voice |
| * think | * interpret input |

The above comparison shows that we are indeed developing multimedia considering ourselves as the ultimate model or the goal.

Mostly, an interactive-video system consists of a PC/AT (or XT), a video player, a monitor for both (or two individual monitors), a keypad to remote-control the video player and an interface between the computer and video.

An interactive videodisc system typically consists of a personal computer (PC), a constant angular velocity (CAV) videodisc player and a television monitor equipped with alternative inputs, e.g., touch screen. Laser-based videodisc system offers the advantages of rapid random access and long-duration still frames without any wear of the disc. A pressed 30 on diameter videodisc played at CAV can store 54000 still video frames on each side which is equivalent to one half hour of real time action. It is possible to plan a presentation by stating the frame numbers and once programmed, the same can be displayed almost instantly and for as long as one likes. In self-learning mode, a learner may branch off to any segment(s) of the disc, back and forth, without loss of time. The computer can determine the needs of the learner and it can either access any frame(s) or it can suggest a possible sequence of learning.

The computer controls the videodisc on the one hand and monitors the students responses and facilitates students' interaction on the other. User-friendliness is accorded high priority. Provision of a touch-sensitive screen is an effective method of seeking student response. Other input devices such as a joystick, mouse, light pen, etc. have not become as popular as the touch screen. Things are so arranged that a device is activated by a student touching it in the same manner as he would in the actual use of the device

An interactive videodisc is perhaps the ultimate in self-paced self-sequenced self-learning which provides immediate response and feedback to the individual learner. The computer may be programmed to propose periodic testing during a learning sequence. In certain cases, it may impose an entry test before commencing a sequence.

Real-time simulations are being increasingly adapted in interactive packages. Examples of simulations are the operation of a power plant, a distillation plant or a laboratory experiment. A learner may control the input and specify the parameters.

He/She may next see the operation of the experiment. Some parameters may be changed at will and the effect of such changes is observed. Further, calibration curves and graphs may be plotted and comparative studies may be undertaken without any difficulty.

A videodisc is normally made from a premaster videotape of very high quality. It may have a large number of still visuals, slides, computer-generated graphics, or moving pictures stored on it. Often a still frame is stored more than once. The technology of preparing visual materials and producing videodisc is fast developing. Many alternative methods of doing so are being explored; some are already available to the end user.

Educational advantages of videodisc include the following:

— greater variety of information.
— attractive modes of presentation,
— immediate access to different content,
— facility for repetition to achieve mastery,
— higher degree of user motivation,
— provision for immediate feedback,
— facility to hold a frame at will, and
— learner-adaptive interactivity.

The only limitation of videodisc has thus far been that the matter is permanently stored on it; it cannot be updated- This limitation has since been overcome with the advent of erasable compact discs. Compact disc (CD) can operate like a blank video cassette and be controlled by a computer. You can record sound picture or text and erase it anytime! Laser operated compact disc is, therefore, a step further than the videodisc.

Interactive Video, i.e., Computer-Based Multimedia has

the following advantages as far as instructional programmes are concerned:

— The instruction consists of carefully engineered learning experiences related to the intended competencies.
— The learner can control the pace, sequence and strategy of learning.
— It involves the learner actively throughout the process of learning.
— It provides drill and practice, problem solving skills, etc. as required.
— It enables the learners to assess their own learning at any state.
— It provides a variety of learning experiences.
— It can employ all the known principles of learning from psychology.

## Teleconferencing

Teleconferencing offers a means of interacting with others at remote places by circumventing travel costs, time and associated problems. Educational applications pertain to communication with groups of learners at different campuses and in different organisations. Management applications are concerned with meetings and seminars. Further applications include information sharing and consultation.

A teleconference is a real-time' interaction between two or more persons at long distances. The technology required to permit teleconferencing is an order of magnitude higher than that for one way process of telecommunications. At present, there are three basic types of teleconferencing systems:

— *Video Conferencing*
— *Audio Conferencing*
— *Computer Conferencing*

In video conferencing, electronic media simulate face-to-face communication using television and audio systems. Audio conferencing is a natural extension of the person-to-person telephone call; to extend to more than two persons. Computer conferencing communicates text and graphics to participants who may access the control computer through typewriter terminals. In a teleconference aimed at total interaction, all three types of media are integrated to supplement one another. A state-of-the-art telecon-ferencing facility would have multi-directional video and audio transmission systems as well as some other means such as document transmittal electronic chalkboard and videotex.

Microcomputers can enable us to be online at a 300 or 1200 baud rate by attaching a modem of the required capacity. Baud rate refers to the speed at which information is accessed or transmitted. Additional equipment needed includes a monitor and a telephone dedicated to the computer or placed in the modem's acoustic coupler plus an optional electronic bulletin board for display. Computer networks-have been known to offer tremendous potential to faculty and students at the university level.

An audio-plus transmission system, also called audiographic system, employs the interactive audio as the basic system supplemented by some form of one-way visual display.

Examples of the audio-plus system are as follows:

— *Electronic chalkboard:* It is a pressure-sensitive surface that converts anything written or sketched into digital information. Remote viewers look at the monitors; they may be able to see chalkboard work as it progresses.
— *Slow-scan television system:* It transmits black-and-white still photographs of real objects, people and visuals at intervals of 15 to 30 seconds.

— *Electronic overhead projection:* It transmits the instructor-drawn graphics to project on overhead projectors for remote learners.
— *Videotex system—Teletext:* Colour pages of digital information with text and graphics is sent to viewers to view it on colour television receivers. A central computer is the key component in such database systems.
— *Document/facsimile transmission* (FAX): Electronic copies of pieces of type-written information is transmitted to all sites to be duplicated as paper handouts.
— *Compressed video:* Selected bits of video information is transmitted to remote television in colour but with limited motion. Full-motion video transmission may also be employed merely to transmit a video programme.

Different configurations of teleconferencing system emerge from the different possibilities of signal transmission:

One-way transmission of electronic signals is called simplex; two-way duplex and one-way at a time in either directions is called half-duplex.

Video conferencing requires duplex transmission to permit two-way movement of audio and video signals. It has massive cost implications. Audio and audio-plus conferencing employing half-duplex transmission across telephone lines constitute more economic and viable means of teleconferencing.

Besides, transmission may be form one point to another, from one point to several points and from several points to the same or to other several points. Simultaneous use of different channels, e.g. telephone lines and satellite or telephone lines and microwave links can result in multidirectional communication. Programme formats may require different teleconferences to be sequential, i.e., one after another or permit one teleconference to be sandwiched into the middle of another. The configuration may be as simple as multi-person connection by telephones or as complex as the transmission of live pictures from several points in a region to the same points as also to several other points.

**Advantages of Teleconferencing**

Some researches on the relative merits of teleconferencing reveal the following advantages:

— Good support for students scattered widely in a region.
— Low cost communication in comparison to travel and other costs.
— Popular mode of instruction where the faculty initiates and controls it.
— Easy scheduling of group discussions and conferencing by telephones and e-mail.
— Immediate feedback from all concerned and quick, remedial actions for.

**Relative Strengths and Weaknesses**

Relative strengths and weaknesses of different types of teleconferencing are tabulated on the next page

**Software Revolution**

Software has lagged behind, more so in the developing countries than in the developed world. A critical analysis of events in the past reveals that greater development effort has gone into hardware. History of film, radio and television in education shows that no software was developed for the film medium, little for radio and only some for television. These media have, therefore, made only marginal impact in teaching and learning. This fact calls for a greater emphasis on the development of software in future. Some countries have resolved to produce and market software in bulk. Such a compromise on quality and an attempt to dump software on others could be detrimental.

**Relative Merits of Different Teleconferencing**

***Audio Teleconferencing***

Audio conferencing is a natural extension of the person-to-person telephone. Good for information exchange where visuals are not necessary. Discussion and exchange, bargaining and negotiations are better conducted by audio communication. It is relatively inexpensive and easy to organise Absence of nonverbal cues may lead to lack of interpersonal feelings.

***Computer Teleconferencing***

It provides written records, and tabulated data. Recorded message is more persuasive than video and less verbose than audio messages. Computer conferencing is more flexible in time and space. It is adaptable for use by individuals at office or at home, for handicapped persons and for delayed use of data for management purposes.

It may, however, be less effective because it cannot enforce participation whereas it requires greater effort to feed information.

***Video Teleconferencing***

More effective than non-visual media particularly where interpersonal communication, graphics and other visuals are concerned. High cost of installation and operation deter its use. Moreover, video conferences with strangers have not proved satisfactory. Educational video conferencing has yet to prove cost-effective.

Cheaper versions such as slow-scan and freeze-frame modes of communication coupled with audio have been more popular.

Software must be produced by groups of people who wish to use them. Why should Ohp transparencies, slides, tape-slide programmes, video/film or even computer software be imported? There may be some reason to get some computer software but no one can make a case for any other. In fact, the secret of the developed world is a coordinated development of hardward and software. They maintain their equipment through preventive maintenance schedule and their manpower is suitably trained to undertake different types of tasks. Software development such as preparation of audiovisual course packages consisting of transparencies, slides and handouts should be subsidised by the government. Groups of faculty members and other specialists may design, produce and employ software in their communication.

It is indeed the turn of the software! Once stocks of visuals are available in different formats, the same can be transferred to the videodisc format for interactive uses.

The latest computer software falls in the category of artificial intelligence. This is called Expert Systems, which operates by simulating an area of expertise into complex structures of mostly the IF-THEN-FLSE variety. The more highly specialised your area of expertise, the more IF-THEN-ELSE structure you have. Each one of these is called a rule. Expert systems have produced spectacular results in science, medicine and engineering. The basic building block of such system is called neuron. There are several types of neurons but each type is akin to an electro-chemical switch. Several billions of neurons connected together in a complex manner are assumed to constitute the brain. Also, several billions of on-and-of patterns appear to constitute the process of thinking! It is the science of Neuron Networks which is leading us into modelling for knowledge-base software.

**Library Assignment**

- Won't you like to learn more about some of the frontier areas in educational technology?
- Look for a good book on interactive video on teleconferencing or some journals in educational technology. Find out the trend of the latest developments and prepare some notes on any one topic.
- Present your findings to your peers and discuss with them, if possible.

**Post-Modular Self-Assessment**

Having gone through the module on the frontiers in educational technology as also other modules in the textbook, you should be aware of the latest developments in the subject. Are You? Why not assess yourself on the following questions? You can't be satisfied with less than 80% score!

| | Questions for Self-Assessment | | | Max. Points | Points Scored |
|---|---|---|---|---|---|
| 1. | State two frontiers in educational technology? | | | 2 | |
| | (a) | (b) | | | |
| 2. | State two recent modes of computer based education | | | 2 | |
| | (a) | (b | | | |
| 3. | What are the main components of an interactive video system? | | | 3 | |
| | (a) | (b) | (c) | | |
| 4. | What is the storage capacity of a videodisc? | | | 2 | |
| 5. | List three plus points of videodisc over video cassette system | | | 3 | |
| | (a) | (b) | (c) | | |
| 6. | Differentiate between video-conferencing and audio-plus conferencing | | | 2 | |
| 7. | Tabulate the relative merits of audio, computer and video conferencing | | | 3 | |
| | Audio | Computer | Video | | |
| 8. | What are the features of the latest software? | | | 3 | |
| | (a) | (b) | (c) | | |
| | | | Total | 20 | |
| | | | Your % Score | | |

## ANSWERS TO SELF-ASSESSMENT QUESTIONS

1. Frontiers in educational technology include interactive video, teleconferencing, knowledge-based software and researches on the teaching-learning process.
2. Computer-based learning, computer-aided instruction, computer-aided classroom teaching and computer-aided evaluation including question-banking, etc.

3. PC AT/XT, Video cassette player/videodisc player, one/two monitors, keypad for controls, interface, etc.
4. A 30 cm (12 inch) diameter videodisc can store 54000 frames on each side; this is equivalent to half an hour real time action.
5. Fast random access, superior still-frame quality, pre-planned lesson presentation, self-learning by selected branching and real time simulation of events.
6. An audio-plus system comprises a two-way audio supplemented by one-way visual display as in electronic chalkboard, slow-scan video, videotex, etc.
7. Good slides and graphics, good computer graphics and animation which can go on videodisc; intelligent and expandable authoring systems and knowledge-based system software.

## Summing Up

Research avenues in educational technology lead us to believe that the audiovisual revolution has taken its roots and the era of self-learning has set in. Computer based instruction, interactive videodisc and teleconferencing and cross-country video-conferencing are some of the near future possibilities. The current twenty first century may usher in new dimensions in educational technology. Welcome?

## QUESTIONS

1. Review analytically the advances in educational technology and throw some light on the frontiers in education technology.
2. Substantiate the statement that Interactive Video and Compact Disc Interactive appear to be the latest educational technologies holding promise in teaching and training by quoting facts and figures.

3. (a) Describe the levels of interactivity on laservision, i.e., levels 0 to 4, and their significance on the development of multimedia vis-a-vis human being.
   (b) List the advantages of interactive video over other media.
4. Explain the concept of teleconferencing with reference to its types, capabilities and educational advantages.
5. (a) Discuss the relative merits of different types of teleconferencing.
   (b) Describe the audio-plus system and give some examples of the same.

# 7

# Learning and Educational Technology

Learning is modification of behaviour as a result of past experience or prior activity. Behavioural modification arising out of learning may be cognitive, affective, sensori-motor or an amalgam of all these in different proportions. Human learning may occur at different levels of complexity. Robert M. Gagne speaks of signal learning at the base and problem-solving are the apex of the hierarchy. Stimulus-response learning of the Skinnerian type, chaining, verbal association, discrimination learning, concept learning and rule learning are the other middle levels in the hierarchy.

Gagne's hierarchy of learning helps the teacher in formulating apt strategies of teaching, taking into consideration the level of learning involved. Often, class instructional objectives may involve a combination of the various categories of learning listed by Gagne. *Signal learning,* the simplest type recognised by Gagne, refers to the mechanical acquisition of conditioned responses of the Pavlovian type exemplified by a dog learning to salivate at the sound of an electric bell after a sequence of bell-food pairings. *Stimulus-Response learning* is akin to the trial-and-error learning conceptualised by the psychologist, E.L. Thorndike, who, through a variety of experiments with white rats in mazes, pointed out that learning involves elimination of incorrect responses and gradual fixation of correct responses with reference to the goal in question (reaching the food in the food box at the centre of the maze) over a period of time and trials. Correct responses leading towards the goal act as positive reinforcers. Such stimulus-response bonds get linked serially as a *chain*, and such a chaining explains the learning of repetitive skills like writing or swimming. When words standing for ideas are joined together to form complex ideas or coherent judgments, we have the next higher category of learning, by *verbal association*. The next higher place of learning involves *discrimination* in which the learner is able to respond disversely to stimuli which, though superficially similar in appearance, are really distinct. *Concept learning* implies a higher level signifying analytical observation of common and essential attributes of a class of objects or ideas leading to unification and generalisation from the data of observation. Concept learning involves and includes the other lower levels of learning. Above this is *rule learning* in which concepts are linked together to stand for universal principles of wide ranging inference and applicability.

The highest level of learning, according to Gagne, is *problem solving,* which is the process of critical thinking and is the basis of new and complex learning. It is the apex of the learning hierarchy in the sense that it involves and is also integrative of the other levels of learning. Problem solving makes use of concepts, associates these in the form of judgments, and the process of problem solving as a tool of learning implies inferences of the deductive and inductive nature. An analysis of even a simple and concrete problem solving situation, like our trying to locate a book which we have misplaced or lost, would indicate how it implies a variety of learning tasks of different levels of complexity, though all these may be telescoped into one another and may not be openly recognisable.

As a corollary of his views on learning, Gagne has listed nine *events of instruction* pertinent to any effective instructional procedure. These events are gaining and controlling attention of pupils, informing the pupils of the expected outcomes of learning in clear and specific terms, stimulating recall of relevant necessary capacities and information on the part of pupils, presenting apt stimuli needed for the learning task, guiding pupil learning, providing feedback and assessing terminal performance, and making provisions for the transferability as well as ensuring retention of learned behaviour. These tasks which look at instruction from the teacher's point of view can be translated into class routine by six possible *modes* of instruction, viz., tutoring, lecturing, recitation, participatory discussion, laboratory and field work and home assignments. These modes of instruction may make use of different *media* such as oral communication, picturs, films etc. In any mode of isntruction, the teacher may utilise one or more media to enhance the nature of communication, retention and innovative application of ideas presented. Educational technology helps in the choice of effective media to suit the instructional mode, which in turn has to be determined taking into consideration the parameters of pupil characteristics, instructional objectives, learning tasks involved as well as the teaching style of individual teachers.

Instruction leading to learning may be in groups or individualised. Individualised programmes consist of learning experiences specifically designed for the individual pupil on the basis of diagnostic procedures employed to determine individual interests and needs. Individual differences which may concern *personality variables* like traits and temperament, *cognitive variables* such as I.Q. and specific abilities, *inquiry variables* like curiosity, experimental attitude, etc., and *sequencing variables* involving random or logical sequencing of instructional information, demand individualisation of learning. Whatever be the level of learning or type of learning, the basic learning, experiences or the *inputs of learning* have to reach the pupil through his senses. As such the senses along with the intellect are vital to learning. In one way senses appear to be even more important than cognitive interpretative abilities for learning as there could be nothing in the intellect which has not been trasmitted through the senses.

Our senses are the gateways to acquiring knowledge. These receptive mechanisms vary in their functions as much as the individuals themselves. The receptive mechanisms feed us the necessary data, the sensory impressions. The natural way of learning by children is principally through the employment of senses. If a now object is given to the child, the child makes sounds with the object, bites it and tastes it, looks at it closely arid slowly learns about the object by making use of its senses. This is the reason for emphasising sense training in Montessori method.

**Sense of Sight**

Of all the senses, sense of sight is most vivid and provides rich experiences to the individual. Nearly 80 per cent of the experiences that a person gains in this world are received through this particular sense. People who have lost the power of this sense, generally compensate to a very large degree by the tactile sense. Impressions created by the sense of sight cannot easily be effaced. A 'visual' will not only attract the attention of pupils but also hold it for as long as it appeals to the sense of sight. Visual experiences are also more effective than verbal experiences. Although the learning process uses the senses as avenues to reach our minds, it is important which sense is used to conduct the message. Experience and research have shown that the following figures are generally valid.

**We Learn**

1.0 per cent through *TASTE*
1.5 per cent through *TOUCH*
3.5 per cent through *SMELL*
11.0 per cent through *HEARING*
83.0 per cent through *SIGHT*

**We Remember**

20 per cent of what we *HEAR*
30 per cent of what we *SEE*
50 per cent of what we *SEE AND HEAR*
80 per cent of what we *SAY*
90 per cent of what we *SAY AND DO.*

**Visual Literary**

The importance and superiority of visual impressions and their interpretation over other sensory channels of information are exemplified today in the stress on what is referred to as *visual literacy.* Visual literacy refers to a group of "vision competencies" one can develop by seeing and at the same time hearing and integrating other sensory, verbal and learning experiences." Visual literacy training, if given to young pupils, will induce motivation and skills in them in expressing themselves first in visual terms and later in spoken and written language. John L. Debes, in explaining the concept of visual literacy, remarks that competencies associated with visual literacy are fundamental to normal human learning. When developed they enable a normally literate person 'to discriminate and interpret the visual actions, objects and symbols that he encounters in his environment'. Through the creative use of these competencies he is able to communicate with others and comprehend, appreciate and master works of visual communication.

The following competencies appear to be involved in

visual literacy: to read visuals with skill, to write with visuals expressing oneself effectively, to be familiar with the look of visual literacy and their use, to appreciate the master works of visual literacy and to be able to translate from visual and verbal language and vice versa. Visual literacy appears to have special benefits not only for those with limited verbal skills but also equally useful for verbally competent and articulate students. The various components of educational technology such as still pictures, drawings, graphics, displays, demonstrations, etc., are all tools and channels of visual literacy.

## Perception and Formation of Concepts

Perception refers "to the way in which man senses or becomes immediately aware of his environment". Although knowledge about the world is gained through the senses, sensory impressions themselves are not enough to give a suitable understanding of the object perceived. It is the brain that receives the impressions and interprets them, which then become organised into meaningful understanding. Thus, any given perceptual event is the result of multiple sensory messages. Perceptual events do not occur in isolation; they are continuous. As a result of constant sensory stimulation, experiences are arranged and rearranged, shuffled and reshuffled, selected and reselected and organised into a convenient combination of patterns. This process finally leads to formation of concept. In general, the understanding of the things and events of the world is based on sensory experiences and the physical objects, as we know them, are products of our own sensory perceptions.

Hence the process of understanding must begin with perception. Or in other words, conceptualisation has its basis in concrete experiences. Where the concrete basis for abstract conceptualisation is lacking, acquisition of the concept by the individual is inadequate or may not take place at all. This is the reason for emphasising maximum concretisation at the lower levels of education so that it will lead to better abstractions in the higher courses. Without a sufficient conceptual foundation, the learning process is impaired and the thinking process is also very much affected.

## Value of One Sense Over Another

A problem may be raised regarding the effectiveness of a particular sense over the others. Actually, our sensory experiences are mixed. When we listen to the teacher, we are not only getting the aural experience but also observe his facial and body gestures. The characteristics of a particular abject may be studied completely by not only making sounds, but also observing its physical features including the weight smell, colour, etc. So long as our sensory mechanisms are functioning normally, we learn quite as readily through one sense as another. The teacher must determine which method of presentation is to be preferred by the particular age-group. The relative values of the various aids must be analysed while deciding to use any one. The aid must make the point clear to the learner interestingly, with economy of time.

## Multi-Sensory Approach

Monotony can be a powerful deterrent to learning. In a typical classroom, we find the teachers talking to an ebullient group of children all the time. It has been recognised that students grasp ideas better through concrete aids like pictures, diagrams, practical work, demonstrations, field trips and the like. In the absence of these various aids that appeal to the senses, children find the school work dull and dreary and hence these may also cause them to drop out of school. Further, to meet the individual differences in a classroom, the teacher must resort to various types of aids that appeal to the different senses. Even among the aids, there are quite a lot of them which appeal to two or more senses simultaneously. For example, while looking at a television programme, or a motion picture, students not only listen but also see. When such aids that appeal to different senses are used, they not only reinforce but also add effectiveness to the teaching procedure.

**Audio-Visual Aids**

Almost every educational reformer has expressed deep concern over the excessive use of words that carry the shadow of meaning but not the substance. Several educationists have struggled to make education realistic. About three centuries ago, J.A. Comenius prepared the first "visualised" textbook which contained some 150 pictures. "Let the pictures be a source of delight to the children and let them become familiar with them before they enter school," was his theory. Later J.J. Rousseau (1712-1778) criticised the teaching of his days and condemned the liberal use of words by teachers. According to him, the teaching process must be directed to the learner's natural curiosity. Rousseau's theory was put into action by Pestalozzi (1756-1827) in his object method'. He became interested in basing instruction on sense perception. Although attempts on the use of concrete aids were made sporadically, intensive development in audio-visual education has started only recently, in the twenties of this century. Educators investigated the possibility of using motion films and by 1929 sound films were being produced. A further impetus to the movement was given daring the World War II when the armed forces suddenly faced teaching tasks of staggering proportions. Today it has been proved beyond doubt by research and classroom experience that audio-visual aids can contribute effectively in teaching.

Audio-visual aids are the different types of tools that appeal to the sense of hearing and vision and are used in classrooms for presentation of abstract information. These materials may be used to convey meaning without complete dependence on verbal symbols or language. Thus, according to definition, a textbook does not fall under the category of audio-visual grouping of instructional materials, but a textbook illustration does. Some audio-visual activities, like going on a field trip, dramatising an event in history, or demonstrating an experiment, are in the nature of process or experiences. Some like motion film or filmstrip need a projector to handle it. Some others, like a chart, a photograph or a picture, need no equipment and can be directly used. Experiences of this type will be classified under visual category. Magnetic tape or disc recordings belong to audio category. Hence the term 'audio-visual aids' designates in common usage both processes and material things. Educators now often refer to the field of audio-visual education as 'educational communication technology', 'audio-visual media', 'learning resources', and 'instructional or educational media'. The terms A.V. materials', 'instructional media' or 'educational media' mean the same thing. All these are implied by the term *Media* generally. More specifically 'media' refers to films, filmstrips, recordings, etc., and programmed instruction, computer assisted instruction, educational. TV are designated as *Methods.*

The replacement of the older and perhaps more familiar term 'Audio-visual materials in education' by the newer term *Educational Technology* or *Instructional Technology* is mainly due to the dynamic expansion of the field of A.V. education and the exciting new developments that promise much more for the future. The main objective of the use of educational technology is the improvement of learning. However, this purpose can be fully achieved only when the vital role of use individual teacher in adding the necessary human, personal factors necessary for the best use of technological hard and software is understood.

## The Fourth Revolution

Eric Ashby (1967) has identified four revolutions in education.

1. The first revolution occurred when societies began to differentiate adult roles and the task of educating the young was shifted, in part, from parents to teachers and from home to *school*.
2. The second was "the adoption of the *written word* as a tool of education". Prior to that time, oral instruction prevailed and it was with reluctance that "writing was permitted to coexist with the spoken word in the classroom."
3. The third revolution came with the invention of *printing* and the subsequent wide availability of bocks.
4. The fourth revolution is the development in *electronics*, notably those involving the radio, television, tape recorder and computer. Behavioural scientists have joined the fourth revolution and have pointed out the importance of defining learning objectives and suggesting ways in which natural learning process can be utilised in the presentation of subject-matter by employing these vast resources.

Educational technology implies a behavioural science approach to teaching and learning in that it makes use of pertinent scientific and technological methods and concepts developed in psychology, sociology, communications, linguistics and other related fields. It also attempts to incorporate the 'management principles of cost effectiveness and the efficient deployment and use of available resources' in men and materials. Educational technology as a concept does not necessarily imply the use of machines and other items of hardware. Experience has shown that more often than not they involve such media, equipment and resources.

In short educational technology, in its wide sense as understood today, includes "the development, application and evaluation of systems, techniques and aids in the field of learning". *As* such its scope encompasses educational objectives, media and their characteristics, criteria for selection of media and resources, management of resources, as well as their evaluation.

The growing use of educational technology in today's schools has helped to release the teacher from the routine role of information giving' so that he can devote his time and effort to the more important tasks of planning, arranging and evaluating learning experiences and outcomes and of encouraging, enthusing, guiding and counselling pupils. The various technological media are used to communicate the needed factual information to pupils and they are capable of doing this perhaps more accurately and efficiently than the teacher. So today 'pupils acquire knowledge through the various media and behavioural changes via the teacher'. Another noticeable trend is the creation of multi-media learning environments in the classroom which involve the use of a variety of interrelated learning experiences. This implies "the selection and use of appropriate sequences of interlinked A.V. or instructional media learning experiences which reinforce and strengthen one another in furthering the progress of the learner."

## The Psychology of Using Teaching Aids

There is an old saying which reads

I hear, I forget;
I see, I remember;
I do, I understand.

### *I Hear, I Forget*

The traditional teacher depended too much on verbal exposition. The pupil hears and forgets. Further, unless the individual has a pragmatic imagination it will be *difficult* for the individual to visualise objects and events, however vivid the verbal description is. It is highly possible that concepts formed will depend upon the nature of background experience of the individual. It is necessary particularly in science and technology that knowledge gained by an individual is accurate, where considerable visualisation of objects and processes is needed and formation of accurate concepts is essential.

### *I See, I Remember*

As a sensory organ, the eye is very highly developed when compared to the other sensory organs. Further, primates and man, due to location of the two eyes in the front of a flat face, have the additional advantage of perceiving depth. This is called binocular vision. The human eye could differentiate very minute differences in colour and shade. It is quite natural that the knowledge gained through the sense of sight is more vivid, accurate and permanent. Hence, what one sees, one remembers. More than 80 per cent of our knowledge is gained through our eyes.

### *I Do, I Understand*

When one is engaged in any practical activity, involving physical work (doing practical work in the laboratory, workshop or in the field) all the senses are used to perceive. Knowledge is through all the senses. Hence inflow of knowledge is through many channels and naturally is quick, complete and more accurate. This is learning by direct experience. Project method involving creative work will provide direct experience in a natural way. (The work has a meaning to the pupil. The outcome is pragmatic. A lot of self activity is involved.) It is an ideal method of making the pupil acquire complete knowledge.

Psychological studies of effective learning emphasise the importance of first-hand concrete experiences involving sensory contacts as the starting point of learning, which later only proceeds towards greater and greater abstraction. A pupil profits most from instruction when he becomes involved through his own interests and purposes and such an involvement is possible when concepts and principles are introduced to him through well-chosen educational media appealing to the different senses. Such a pupil will also act creatively. The teacher of today has at his command an array of aids, some ready made and some fabricated, by the teacher. Using these teaching aids, the teacher can plan learning situations and be sure of realising his objective. The teacher can make use of specific audio-visual aids to suit his purpose. The aids being *concrete* will be able to secure the attention of the pupils, motivate, enable the pupils form accurate *concepts,* ensure *permanent retention* of the knowledge gained. A teacher using appropriate aids can make clear a difficult concept even to a below-average pupil very easily.

The activities during a class session should be varied to prevent boredom, purposeful for effectiveness and pre-planned to achieve the set objective. The teacher to effect maximum learning should make the pupils look, listen and think. He should secure their attention and maintain the same throughout. Interest should be created and learning should be speeded up, fixed and consolidated. Knowledge gained should be transferable and utilitarian. The teacher of today makes sure of all the above outcomes by making use of the right type of A.V. aids at the right time in the right way.

The teacher should use verbal exposition, which is the least effective method of imparting instruction, to a minimum extent, supplementing the same with judicious use of proper teaching aids and providing ample direct experience where knowledge is gained through multi-sensory media.

## Media and Methods of Teaching

The teacher practitioner is often puzzled when he is introduced to the many types of audio-visual aids available to him. Too often the novice in the art of teaching looks upon the hardware of educational technology as a convenient substitute for professional planning and competency. So, even at the outset, it should be made clear to the young teacher that different media and methods are suitable for realising different learning outcomes, that the effectiveness of aids depends not only on the material provided but also on the techniques used and that the ability and resourcefulness of the teacher is as important in the classrooms of today as it was in the traditional classrooms. For some instructional objectives the chalkboard will suffice: for some others a brief lecture correlated with a suitable and simple demonstration will be enough; while for realising certain other learning outcomes the overhead projector or the sound film projector may be apt. "As new devices are developed, it is quite common for each to be heralded as the panacea for educational ills." The overhead projector, the teaching machine and the educational TV have all had their day. However, the fact remains that the teacher must determine how each device can uniquely serve his specific teaching needs.

Competence in the art and craft of classroom instruction requires mastery of many methods and modes of communicating information and influencing pupil's behaviour. These include not only the special techniques associated with the teaching of specific subjects but also general organisational strategies needed for running the classroom: keeping order, facilitating communication, catering to individual differences among pupils, etc. New instructional methods develop from different sources such as psychological research, pedagogical theory, academic disciplines, outgrowth of teacher's ideas and experiences, impressions of how learning ought to occur. Whatever be the source and whatever be the nature of instructional method adopted, A.V. media help to support and supplement the teacher's work. Only, the teacher should not relinquish his responsibilities and believe in the view "let multimedia do it", as meagre/negative results mayh be there without proper planning, supervision, and follow-up.

## Integrated Use of Teaching Aids

Teachers, while planning their instructional strategy, have to select the most suitable teaching aid or aids, sometimes even designing and fabricating them if not readily available. The following steps indicate the flow in procedure for use of aids most suitable for promoting the desired learning outcomes in pupils: (a) awareness of intended learning outcomes and definition of these in observable behavioural terms; (b) selection of apt and suitable aids taking into consideration the following—entry behaviour of pupils, anticipated terminal behaviour of pupils, the strength of the class (small groups—about 25-30 pupils and large groups—more than 30), materials readily available and facilities available for fabrication of needed or innovated aids, facilities available in the classroom for using these (e.g., hanging facilities for charts, darkening facilities, power supply, projection screen, ventilation etc. If a projected aid is planned for use); (c) getting ready for use the chosen aid or aids; (d) deciding upon the commentary to be given while using these aids and the specific aspects to be kept in view; (e) deciding upon the questions to be posed and other evaluation procedures to be used and (f) deciding upon the follow-up work to be given to pupils for consolidating the resulting learning outcomes and to enable the pupils to apply the knowledge gained to real-life situations, through assignments, construction projects etc. While using aids, the pupils should be informed as to *what* to observe. Similarly, when a demonstration is conducted the pupils should be trained to observe it, posing to themselves such questions as *what* is happening? *When* does it happen? *Why* does it happen? etc. A good teacher, even while Planning any lesson, should think of the teaching aids to be used and get them ready; such integrated use of teaching aids results in making class instruction dynamic and effective.

Summing up, it can be said that instructional efficiency is enhanced by the use of appropriate media, and the teacher, to get the best out of media, has to exercise his judgement and innovative skills in his choice. The first step in such an exercise is perhaps to eliminate media that may not, for one reason or other, suit the teacher's purpose, and then make a specific choice of suitable medium or media based on rational considerations from among those left over. When more than one medium is chosen for a unit of instruction, the use of these has to be suitably coordinated while planning instruction. In media selection the structure of the subject matter as well as the specific objectives of instruction form the basis of selection. These, coupled with such factors as the teacher's skill in adaptability and innovation, and the entering characteristics of the pupils, help in media selection. The class size is also a constraint as certain media are suitable only for use with small groups. Other factors such as time available, classroom material facilities; availability of media as well as its cost effectiveness, suitability of software in terms of specific teaching goals, also have to be borne in mind. Media only help in expanding and enlarging the influence of the human element in education and the role of the teacher continues to be a central factor in the instructional process in spite of the tremendous potentialities of educational hard and softwares.

## Dale's Cone of Experience

Human beings derive all the experiences are mainly from three sources, namely (i) direct sensory contact which involves *doing,* (ii) pictures or some other forms of representation of objects which involve *observing,* and (iii) oral or printed words which involve *symbolising.* Of these three possibilities, the third is perhaps of least value from the point of view of teaching the young learner. All the learning experiences which on be utilised for classroom teaching are shown by Edgar

Dale in a pictorial device—"pinnacle form"—which he called the "Cone of experience". If we travel up the pinnacle from its base, every thing has been arranged in the order of increasing abstractness or decreasing directness. The experiences included in the cone are as indicated below.

1. *Direct, purposeful experience* that is seen, handled, tasted, felt, touched and smelt, i.e., the experience that is gained through the senses. These experiences are not only direct but are also purposeful. Purposeful means that the experiences are active with a purpose. "An ounce of experience is better than a tonne of theory, simply because it is only as an experience that any theory has vital and verifiable significance." Objects are the reality. Hence they are preferred in teaching provide the means to establish correct initial concepts in the minds of pupils. Specimens are excellent visual aids but they cannot be a substitute for the real object as they are only a sample or part of an object.

2. *Contrived experience* It is like a working model, which is an editing of reality and differs from the original either in size or in complexity: The simplification of the real object becomes necessary when the real thing cannot be perceived directly. The real object may be too big or too minute; may be obscured or confused or concealed. In such circumstances, the limitation is preferred for better and easier understanding.

3. *Dramatic participation* is one in which certain real events of the past are represented so that we can get as close as possible. Dramatisations are available in a variety of forms. There are the carefully rehearsed full-length plays, complete with costumes and scenery. Puppet shows, pageants, pantomimes, tableaux, dialogues, spontaneous acting and mock conventions are other forms of drama. In each of these activities, one can be an observer or a participant. The experience is more meaningful when one actively participates in the dramatisation than when one merely watches. The observer

is not compelled to 'feel like' the character whereas the actor must try to 'become' the character that he portrays. His appearance on the stage must be dramatic in the sense that it must be stirring, compelling attention and making a strong emotional impact on the audience. Proper costume definitely heightens effect of dramatisation in three ways:

1. It compels attention.
2. It helps to identify the actor—young, old, type of work or profession of the character.
3. It enables the actor to feel and play his role better.

Types of dramatised experiences include the following:

*The Play*

This kind of drama vividly portrays important ideas related to social problems.

*The Pageant*

This is a kind of community drama, usually based on local history.

*Pantomime*

In pantomime, the effect depends upon the movements of the actors, for they do not speak.

*Tableau*

This is a picture-like scene. The movements of the characters are restricted and they stand still, silently.

*Puppets*

These present ideas with extreme simplicity, without elaborate scenery or costume. Puppet show has mass appeal and is used to great advantage at all levels of education. Shadow puppets, simple rod puppets, hand puppets and stringed puppets or marionettes are the different types of puppetry.

4. *Demonstration experiments:* Certain complicated processes can be performed by the teacher for the benefit of pupils who are reduced to the position of passive observers. The demonstrations may be set up on a demonstration table which is usually kept in an elevated place so that all can closely watch the demonstrations. In the lecture-demonstration approach such demonstrations are interwoven with the lecture.

5. *Field trips:* This forms the connecting link between the school and the community. Numerous opportunities with an extensive array of materials are offered by the community which could very well be utilised for teaching. The extent to which these resources should be used will depend upon their potential usefulness in supplementing the classroom teaching. This technique is unique in that the pupils gain first-hand experiences with the things and phenomena which cannot be brought into the classroom. Only when this is not possible, the teacher should have recourse to other visual aids. But in our present system of mass education this is quite impossible to arrange too often.

6. *Exhibitions and museums:* When it is not feasible to go out into the community, it becomes exceedingly important that we bring the outside world into the classroom by means of exhibits and concrete representation of things. The science department of every school should have a museum. The natural instinct for collecting and hoarding found in school children, should be mobilised in building the museum. A well-developed museum is not only an asset to that school but also a motivating and vitalising factor for the particular subject.

7. *Television:* Television can bring a dimension beyond the range of motion pictures. It can bring the real event as it actually happens. In the case of motion film, the event has already been filmed and hence the outcome is known. But in

a telecast, the event is seen as it unfolds with the outcome uncertain. The television telecast is often 'history in the making.'

8. *Motion pictures:* they are increasingly being used by teachers nowadays. If these are carefully prepared and properly used in the classroom, the results that are obtained are quite comparable with those of ordinary teaching. Motion pictures with sound system would yield good results in teaching all the subjects in the school curriculum.

9. *Radio and recordings:* The advantages of radio as an educational aid are quite numerous and its functioning as "one way communication" which is a drawback, has been overcome to some extent by means of recordings which can be played and the reactions of the pupils observed.

10. *Still pictures, pictures, illustrations, stereographs, sides filmstrips* and *micro projections:* These can be either projected on a screen by means of projection machines and accessory equipment of given for individual study.

11. *Designed materials:* Maps, charts, graphs, diagrams and cartoons when properly employed tend to promote a keener interest and a better understanding of concepts.

12. *Verbal symbols:* This is the usual 'chalk and talk' method which requires great thinking. The word, or idea of concept or scientific principle expressed here a distinction should be made between the written and spoken word. According to linguistics, the spoken word is primary and printed word is secondary. "Printed words are only the symbols for symbols. Jesperson says that "A written word is mummified and someone imparts life to it by transposing it mentally into the corresponding spoken word. Hence the spoken word should be placed lower than the written word in the cone.

It can thus be seen that the opportunities afforded by the sensitive aids are very great and that it all depends upon the ingenuity of the teacher as to how he could exploit the learning situation by the right use of the proper aid. Nevertheless, the richer the teaching materials, the more will be the teacher's responsibility to correlate and plan his teaching. The following *general principles* may however serve as guides to the use of these aids.

1. There are three stages in a learning process when an educational aid is used to supplement the ordinary teaching, viz., (i) preparing the pupils for the learning experience, (ii) reinforcing the values while the pupils are sharing the experience, and (iii) relating the experience with the lesson and thus stimulating further learning.
2. The aids must be adapted to the intellectual maturity of the pupils and to the nature and extent of their previous experience.
3. There is no best aid which has all the advantages. Most visual aids suffer from some psychological limitations. The teacher should be familiar with the advantages and limitations of the various types of sensory aids.
4. Visual aids should not be considered as substitutes for oral and written methods of acquiring knowledge. They should be used to supplement the classroom teaching.
5. Visual instruction in the classroom should not be confused with entertainment. The effective use of an aid depends primarily on careful planning by the teacher.
6. In all cases, the time and effort on the use of a particular aid in preference to others must always be justified.

## A Practical Cone Classifying Different Aids

The 'Cone' proposed by Edgar Dale was the earliest attempt

to classify the audio-visual aids according to their effectiveness in communicating ideas. The cone classifies sensory aids in terms of greater or less concreteness and abstractness as learning experiences. The cone device should not be construed as an accurate arrangement of the learning experiences systematically from base to pinnacle. Field trip has been classified as an experience involving only observation and hence has been placed much high in the ladder. Actually, field trip provides rich, first-hand experience in some instances and hence should be classified under 'Direct, purposeful experience'. Similarly, projected aids are considered to be more effective in teaching than the non-projected aids. But projected aids occupy a top position in the pinnacle, signifying thereby that they are comparatively abstract experiences in relation to direct experience. Figure 1 depicts a practical cone classifying different aids with reference to their relative effectiveness.

# 8

# Environmentalism as a Teaching Technique

## What?

We are living in an era where we are beginning to see the catastrophic results of industrialism on the environment and are now living the effects - acid rain, the greenhouse effect, endangered species (we soon may be one of them), the destruction of the forests, drinking water and fertile ground. We have treated the earth like a giant garbage dump and there is no more room for the garbage. Everyone needs to be environmentally responsible NOW. We can begin by living an environmentally responsible life in the classroom.

## How?

1. Students should be informed about the potentially devastating effects of the North American lifestyle. Thus, the teacher must also be informed. If students realise the effects of waste and pollution, their efforts to deter these effects will have meaning to them.
2. The teacher should establish a new "Three-R's" rule for the classroom - Recycle, Reuse and Reduce.
3. Paper-Just think for a moment, about the amount of paper that fills the wastepaper baskets of classrooms. The teacher should provide a container for recyclable paper to be collected. Teachers should band together

to lobby against schools using paper that is NOT from recycled materials.

4. Students should be encouraged to bring things from home which would not be recycled there. Tin cans are great for holding water for using waterpaints, newspapers are always welcome and needed in art classes.

## FAMILY TREES

**What?**

All families have a history that is unique and important to their members. By having students draw their family trees they get a sense of how far back in history their families can be traced. They also develop a tie with family members (alive or deceased) whom they have never met. The family tree is a representation of the family. It can include dates of birth and death, pictures or just names. The student's name is placed at the bottom of the tree, representing the trunk along with brothers and sisters. Parents on corresponding "branches" and parents' parents above that and so on. Making of a family tree is popular at the elementary level.

**How?**

1. Students should be shown an example of a family tree. The teacher may want to construct and share his/her family tree as an example.
2. The teacher should explain how the names are placed and how placing the names correctly shows the relationships between/among family members.
3. If students are able, allow them to draw their own trees. Younger students may require teacher-prepared family tree outlines.
4. The teacher should then encourage students to interview their parents and grandparents to find out about their ancestors. Teachers should ask students

to find out about their ancestors and the time period in which they lived.

5. Enough time should be given to students to fill in their trees. The teacher should constantly monitor progress and offer assistance when required.
6. Opportunity should be given students to share their trees with their peers. Students should be invited to talk about their family members. The teacher may arrange to have a grandparent as a special visitor to talk to students about his/her life.
7. Completed family trees may be colourfully displayed.

**Important Guidelines**

1. Evaluation criteria must be dearly defined.
2. A trip to the 'local history room' of the local library or archives is an interesting supplement to the study of family history.

## FILLING OUT FORMS

**What?**

Students can practice filling out such forms such as income tax, wills and cheques which they will be required to fill out accurately in their adult lives. By giving students the opportunity to fill out these forms when they are young they will be prepared to fill them out when they have to. This exercise also gives students insights into the workings of the organisations/businesses which require such forms. Students improve skills of inquiry and critical thinking by considering the usefulness of the form and the appropriateness or inappropriateness of some forms (i.e. religion, marital status).

**How?**

1. The teacher should attempt to acquire many copies of the actual form to be filled out. Banks will usually

provide blank cheques, deposit slips, and other forms for a nominal fee.

2. The teacher should give a brief introduction to the purpose of the form. Encourage students to brainstorm for ideas. The teacher should then show students an example of a filled out form and go through it step by step. The teacher should proofread for accuracy prior to the introduction.
3. The teacher should encourage and ask questions at this point.
4. Students are then given forms to fill out. They should be reminded to think about what is being asked and why. Is it relevant?
5. If the exercise is being done during class time, the teacher should visit each student as he/she completes the form. Students should always be concerned about accurate spelling.
6. If students will be doing it as a homework assignment, remind them about accuracy and appropriateness of questions. If they feel that they should not be required to divulge certain information, then they should be required to defend their position.
7. The teacher should be clear on his/her expectations. Let students know how they will be evaluated. It is common in this type of exercise to require 100% accuracy. Students should know this.

**Important Guidelines**

1. A collection of completed forms should be kept by students in a scrapbook for reference.
2. If the "real world" requires total accuracy on a given form, then the teacher should require the same.
3. The teacher may want to supplement this exercise with a field trip to the appropriate business/organization.

4. Most forms will have to be filled out in ink. Students should be allowed to practice before being evaluated for 100% accuracy.
5. The teacher may want to consider having an "expert" visit the class and explain the forms (i.e. bank manager).
6. In the information age, we are constantly being bombarded with forms and documents. It is a good idea to prepare students at an early age - not just to fill out forms accurately but to critically evaluate forms and documents when they are associated with them.
7. The students should know WHY they must learn to fill out various forms. In other words, the students should understand the teacher's objectives and expectations. The teacher should ask himself/herself the following questions when preparing objectives:
   (a) What forms will most students be required to fill out during their lifetimes?
   (b) How will I integrate form filling exercises into the regular curriculum?
   (c) Will students learn anything about business, the community, the government or society by examining and filling out forms?
   (d) How will filling out forms enhance the total learning experience?
   (e) Can any interesting and exciting activities be developed from working with forms?
   (f) How can the teacher best prepare the students for the adult world?

## FILMSTRIPS

### What?

Filmstrips can be projected on a large screen for a group or they can be viewed by individual students on mini-viewers.

Still pictures are projected and may or may not have written captions. Some filmstrips come with audio tapes or records with pre-recorded commentaries which accompany the visuals. Filmstrips may be used for large groups or individualised instruction, for introducing a unit or for teaching a lesson.

**How?**

1. Decide when would be the most suitable time to show the filmstrip. Topical filmstrips should be closely linked to the content material being studied/and should not be shown in isolation. If filmstrips need to be ordered, make sure this is done well in advance.
2. Once the filmstrip is in the teacher's possession, preview it. If the filmstrip has audio accompaniment, preview the filmstrip with and without it. The teacher may discover that the audio accompaniment is less than stimulating. Uninteresting, monotone audio can spoil exciting visuals.
3. If the teacher decides that he/she will be the voice of the filmstrip, plan what will be said. This is a great opportunity to stimulate discussion. Develop questions to ask the students. Moreover, this open-ended approach is more creative.
4. Ensure that all audio and video equipment is working properly.
5. Show the filmstrip. Relate the content of the filmstrip to course content where appropriate.
6. After the filmstrip is viewed, review and reflect on important points of the filmstrip.

**Important Guidelines**

1. Use non-captionalised filmstrips whenever possible. With this type of filmstrip, students rely on their own ability to interpret pictures without being influenced by prepared, "authoritative" text.

2. Relate the content of the filmstrip to tie content of the unit under study. Make reference to filmstrips students have seen when appro-priate. Filmstrips are not made to be watched and then forgotten so the teacher must make the experience an exciting one.
3. Teachers should budget for preparation time (including previewing the filmstrip).
4. Students are increasingly becoming accustomed to fast moving high-tech productions and may be bored with filmstrips.

## FLAGS

### What?

The use of flags as a teaching technique usually involves using the flag, the emblem of a country or province, as a resource to learn about a particular country or province and its people and culture. When we think of a flag we usually picture a colourful cloth banner representing a country. Flags, however, came into existence a long time ago and were not necessarily made of cloth. Wooden or metal symbols were carried by ancient Egyptian and Roman armies as they proceeded onto battle in ceremonial processions and hunting expeditions. Ancient flags or symbols had various meanings and some were given the power of an omen. In medieval Europe, for example, the fall of a flag signalled or predicted defeat in battle. Other symbols used to identify a people and a territory like totem poles or war paint are *not* flags.

### How?

1. During the study of a particular country and/or its people the teacher should include the study of the flag of that particular country as it reveals relevant information about the people and the politics of the

country. The teacher should first present the flag or a representation thereof to the students.

2. Students should be given adequate time to become familiar with the details of the flag. Having students draw and colour the flag is an effective and active way to learn the details about the flag. Students should consider the following questions during their study of flags:
   (a) When did the flag become an official symbol of the territory? Who designed the flag? Why do you think the flag was designed in a particular way?
   (b) What does each design on the flag represent? What colours are used? Why do you think these particular colours were used?
3. Students should be given the chance to brainstorm ideas as to what the details of the flag represent Students should be given some back-ground information about the culture to aid them in their analysis.
4. Time should also be devoted to the study of the history of a given flag thus revealing the history of a people. The study of the flag should also include the study of the meaning and effect of a flag on people. For example, the American flag is such an important symbol to the American people that it is illegal to drag an American flag on the ground or to fly a tattered flag.

## Important Guidelines

1. Studying flags does not mean memorising in order to identify the flag of a particular country. It involves the study of the people who live under the flag.
2. Students should not be required to memorise the details of all the flags of the world without doing

activities which concern the people which the flag represents. A separate and distinct unit on flags could be successfully taught but it should include some discussion of the human side of the flag.

3. Sometimes, the teacher may devote intensive study to one particular flag - the flag of the country the students and teacher live in. Consequently, little or no time is devoted to the study of flags of other nations. This technique is not conducive to globalism and should be avoided.
4. The teacher should have a purpose in mind for including the study of flags. A set of objectives will need to be determined. The teacher may consider the following:
   (a) The student will identify the flags of various countries, provinces, countries or organisations (to be decided by the teacher).
   (b) The student will make thoughtful hypotheses about the meanings behind the colours and symbols on flags.
   (c) The student will complete a variety of activities concerning people and cultures represented by flags.
   (d) The student will design a flag representing himself/herself and/ or his/her family.
5. Studying flags the global way is time consuming. The teacher may opt to set up a learning centre on flags of the world.
6. Along with the flag, heraldry of a country or province can also be used as a teaching technique.

## FLASHCARDS

### What?

Flashcards are popular in the elementary school - most teachers use them in Mathematics. They can however be suitably used in teaching social studies, history, science, and languages. History cards, geography cards, fact cards, concept cards, important people cards, are commonly used in the schools. Knowledge games have also popularised the use of flashcards in the last decade. Flashcards are useful as they allow factual (sometimes conceptual) information to be learned in an enjoyable fashion. Flashcards can be handily used by individuals, by partners or by the whole class. Flashcards can be used by the teacher to provoke discussion or to assist students in feeling what it is like to be put in a new or different situation.

The use of flashcards is an excellent technique for individuals because it provides the instant feedback through the self-checking device on the back of the card.

### How?

1. Teachers should decide what particular skills or knowledge the flash-cards should be used to portray.
2. Students can use the flashcards individually.
3. Students can take turns reading the questions to one another and also reading the answers from the backside.
4. Teachers should prepare flashcards to fit into the particular unit of study. Many different kinds of flashcards are also commercially available.
5. It is a valuable activity for students to make (and write) their own set of cards.
6. Before making flashcards, teachers have to conduct some research into specific types of information, such

as important people or facts that fit into the topic or the unit of study.

7. It is easy to use 71/2cm x 12 cm recipe cards or cards cut from a bristle board. Cards could be colour coded - different topics can be highlighted through different colours.
8. Questions written on the front should be short, clear and precise. Answers are written on the back. Just like the various kinds of knowledge games that are available in the market, the teacher should try to write questions at various levels of thinking (Bloom's Taxonomy).
9. Flashcards should be stored in an area where they are easily accessible to students.
10. Instructions/directions should be posted so that students know when and how to use flashcards, and how to put them away after use.
11. It is suggested that flashcards could be effective for teaching current events (for instance to review the cardinal events of the past year/ decade/century). Students may find it interesting to prepare these flash cards from newspapers/magazines or other sources.

**Important Considerations**

1. Allow students to prepare their own flashcards.
2. Teachers should be cautious about the questions. Questions should be clear, concise and at different levels of thinking.
3. The teacher should use a variety of flashcards and vary the content of each set to avoid boredom.
4. The flashcard technique should not be over used.

## FOLK SONGS

**What?**

Folk songs, historical and usually culture specific, provide us with valuable information about people and history. Folk music is the song of the common people. It provides insight into the interests, attitudes, values and beliefs of a particular people during a particular time.

**How?**

1. Get students involved in the process of learning from folk songs.
2. Give students some background information (i.e. of the culture and/ or country).
3. If at all possible the teacher should learn to play and/ or sing the folksong so that he/she can help the students to learn.
4. Dissect the folksong by forming hypotheses as to why the song was written, played and sung; how the words and/or music reveal information about the people who perform it; what instruments are involved and/ or what the purpose of the song is.
5. The songs studied must be authentic and students should be given the words to the songs on paper.
6. When all necessary *background information is given, all audio equipment has been checked, a purpose for listening to the folksong as been established and students are attentive,* let them listen to the song for the first time. Encourage singing along and clapping. The students will have an opportunity to analyze the song second time around. The teacher must not take the fun out of such an exercise.

Important considerations:

1. Information about costumes and dance relating to individual folk-songs is an exciting and interesting supplement to any culture-related unit.
2. Children oftenhave vivid imaginations. The teacher should encourage students to use them. Given some motivation and encouragement, thestudents will often come up with all the necessary historical information required by listening carefully and using their imaginations.
3. The teacher should have some prior knowledge about the song and its history so that any false notions canbediscussed and dismissed.

# 9

# Teaching Technology: Discovery and Diffusion

Of late, the techniques of revitalising classroom teaching in Indian schools has been paid a food deal of attention. Basic education is intended to revolutionise all life and activity in the primary schools and draw out 'the best in the child—body, mind and spirit. The Secondary Education Commission devoted an entire chapter in its report to dynamic methods of teaching, discussing the objectives of the apt and right techniques, the values of various activity methods and the different ways in which these methods and techniques could be adapted to suit different levels of intelligence. Considerable efforts have been made during the last decades through seminars, workshops, refresher courses and summer institutes to introduce the teacher, especially at the secondary stage, to new techniques of instruction. The use of audio-visual aids has been on the increase in urban as well as in rural schools, and even television has been brought into the service of classroom teaching in many big cities. Despite that it will be generally agreed that the impact of these activities on teaching practices in the vast majority of our schools has not been very significant yet. The picture is particularly dismal in the rural areas, and especially in the elementary schools. In the average school today, instruction still conforms to a conventional mechanical routine, continues to be dominated by the old besetting evil of verbalism and therefore remains as dull and uninspiring as before.

Why does this happen? The problem is complex and the answers to it are not easy to give. But in our opinion, the following are the four major factors that impede progress:

1. *The failure to develop proper educational research on teaching methods.* Little has been done to find out in crucial sectors the methods that are best suited to our conditions and needs. For instance, the best methods teaching beginning reading in a phonetic script like Devanagri have yet to be developed.
2. *The weakness of the average teacher.* By and large, the competence of the average teacher is poor; this general education is below standard and his professional preparation unsatisfactory.
3. *The rigidity of the existing educational system.* Better methods of teaching are discovered, not so much through educational research, as through the adventures of gifted teachers who have the courage to get off the beaten track. Our educational system is not designed to encourage initiative, creativity and experimentation on a large scale and is, therefore, not able to keep itself abreast of the times.
4. *The failure of the administrative machinery to bring about a diffusion of new and dynamic methods of teaching.* Even assuming that a good method of teaching is discovered and is actually introduced in a few progressive schools, the problem still remains of diffusing it among the other schools so that it becomes the common practice in the educational system as such. This is a difficult task, and we have yet to find the right techniques for accomplishing it.

We do not propose to examine here the methods of teaching different school subjects as there is a good deal of pedagogical literature available on these topics. It is our considered opinion, however, that the failure to modernise our teaching methods is very largely due to the third and fourth factors stated above—the rigidity of the educational system and the administrative failure to diffuse even known and practised methods among the schools.

## Elasticity and Dynamism

In all modern societies where the rate of change and of the growth of knowledge is very rapid, the educational system should be elastic and dynamic. It must give freedom to its basic units—the individual pupil in a school, the individual teacher among his colleagues, and the individual school (or cluster of schools) within the system to move in a direction or at a pace which is different from that of other similar units within the system without being unduly hampered by the structure of the system as a whole. In this process, the freedom of the teachers is the most vital; it is almost synonymous with the freedom of the school, for the pupils can rarely be freer than the men and women who teach them. It will, therefore, be quite an order to equate the elasticity and dynamism of an educational system basically with the freedom of teachers.

It is worth remembering that advances in classroom practice never occur on a broad front, with all the teachers and all the schools moving forward in unison. In a school system with a large number of untrained or postly trained teachers, there is need for a solid framework of detailed syllabuses, text-books, examinations, well-defined rules and frequent inspections. The average teacher who wants security rather than opportunity for creativity may welcome his support. But the work of the best teachers can be crippled if they are not permitted, enthused and helped to go beyond the departmental prescriptions. The success of an educational reform will depend upon this flexible approach where the good school or the good teacher is able to forge ahead and the necessary supports are provided to the weaker institutions to introduce the reform gradually. The task of the administrator or inspector in such a situation becomes very difficult. He cannot take the easy line of imposing common restrictions on all or be daring enough to give equal freedom to all. We expect him to analyse the strengths and weaknesses of each school and of each school teacher and to help them make the best progress they can. For making an educational system elastic and dynamic, the administrator should develop this competence, to discriminate between school and school, between teacher and teacher, and to adopt a flexible mode of treatment for individual or institutions at different levels or" development. This alone can help teachers to promote initiative, creativity and experimentation.

Some definite general conditions are compulsory to promote this elasticity and dynamism. Some of the significant of which are given hereunder:

1. The individual teacher is most likely to try bold changes in teaching practice if there is a feeling of reform in the air and if he sees his small contribution as part of a major social revolution.
2. The experimenting teacher must have much more than the passive acquiescence of the school inspectors. He must feel that officers of the Education Department are personally eager to see experimentation and that they are willing, within reasonable limits, to accept a proportion of failures as part of the price.
3. The inspectors are *Authority*, present and obvious. They should be consulted from the beginning should know that their criticism and suggestions carry weight, and should be made to feel that the proposed changes

are, in some measure, *their* reforms. A school system can be no more elastic or dynamic than the inspectors will let it be. This is why the in-service education of inspecting officers assumes great significance in recent years.

4. The sympathy and support of principal and senior teachers must be won quite early in the programme if they are not to dampen all youthful ardour to experiment and explore. They may not want to break new ground themselves. But if they do not feel they are being ignoted and that the new system is not being foisted on them, they can become its patrons, if not its practitioners. There is also much to be gained by winning the approval of teachers' organisations to any movement that increases flexibility in the school system. Individuals will experiment more readily if they feel that experimentation has the general support of the profession.
5. The strengthening of the teacher's sense of inner security is a purpose common to all the methods advocated to increase the elasticity or dynamism in a school system. It is the basis of all real reform in teaching practice. Anything that breaks down the isolation of the teacher increases his sense of assurance and makes it easier for him to adventure. There are occupations where a mass advance can be achieved by the invention of new equipment and the issuing of instructions for its use. No worth-while advance in is possible teaching method unless the individual teacher understands what he is doing and feels secure enough to take the pioneering new steps beyond the bounds of established practice. It is easier for a teacher to do so in a small group than when he is working alone. The success of 'team teaching' in introducing new teaching techniques into some American schools is

based on the fact that *it is not the individual but the team that is responsible for the planning and execution of new methods.* It is believed that the proposed organisation of a school complex in which the teacher works in a cooperative group is more likely to help flexibility than the present system of isolation and segregation.

6. Nothing diminishes a teacher's sense of security or his willingness to take advantage of freedom so seriously as does his ignorance of the subject-matter he has to teach. If he is only a few lessons ahead of his class he dare take no risks, and finds safety in the old routine of rote memorising. The teacher's general education level increase is, in general, the surest way of ensuring that some of them will adopt livelier and more meaningful methods of teaching. Fortunately, the limiting factors is not so much the absolute amount of knowledge the teacher has but the gap between what he knows and what his pupils know. Resultantly, the easiest place to introduce innovations is in classes I and II. There is also a great advantage in taking the lowest classes of the schools as a starting point for reform, since it is at this level that the greatest 'pupil wastage' occurs through dropouts and repetition.
7. In the state of doubt, teachers will teach in the way they were taught themselves and not in the way they were told to teach. So, if a school system is to become more flexible and teaching methods more lively and varied, it is essential that these qualities be established very early in the practice, as well as in the theory, of at least some of the teacher-training institutions. A few training institutions at both the primary and the secondary levels should become nodal centres for devising, testing, and adapting methods and materials to be used.

8. A institution or teacher will be able to introduce innovations more easily if the pupils' parents know enough about their purpose so as not to have any fear that they will interfere with their children's opportunities at the final examination. A strong and respected head-master or teacher can probably best win over the parents by his own efforts; but in most cases, it will be neccessary for the Department to help in convincing parents that changes in methods are desirable and officially approved.
9. More likely innovations are to occur if there is a proper and well regulated ladder of promotion up which the brigh young teacher can hope to climb by outstanding service.
10. Apparently, elasticity or dynamism will be increased if there is a reasonable provision of books, teaching materials, and services that will enable some children to undertake part of their work alone or in groups. There is a limit to what can be expected of the most imaginative teacher if all he has is a bare room, a blackboard, a standard textbook, and fifty pupils. The most pressing needs for a teacher who wants to branch out on new methods are, therefore, a good supply of books and paper, and particularly at the lower levels of school education, some simple tools and materials for making equipment. If some teachers in the more poorly equipped schools are to have a real opportunity to make use of any freedom they are given, it would seem desirable to have at the disposal of the district education officer a sum of money, not too tightly bound up by regulations, that might be used, with discrimination, in providing the minimum facilities and services to certain schools and teachers who show a special willingness and capacity to adopt new

methods and standards of teaching. The amount of such aid should never be so great as to make any experiment expensive, unreal, and incapable of being applied widely. Too many 'pilot projects' are conceived on such an elaborate scale that they irritate teachers in the average schools and are of little value to the system as a whole.

The like measures, elaborated above, if can be taken, schools and teachers will have opportunities to voluntary venture forth on their own and try out new ideas and experiments. Of course, those that win actually utilise this freedom will be few. But it is these few teachers and schools whose work will put dynamism into the system as a whole and help in raising standards, in breaking new ground and in continually adapting the system to the demands of a changing society of present day.

### *New Methods' Diffusion*

Of course, elasticity in a school system is obviously of limited value unless the good practices developed by a few adventurous teachers or schools are spread more widely through the system as a whole. Lamentingly, this is by no means an automatic process in education, where successful experiments frequently die with the men and women who started them, and where the natural rate of spread of even more viable innovations is measured in decades rather than in years. It takes a great deal of administrative skill and perseverance to get bold new methods understood and accepted he the body of average and below average teachers, even when they have amply proved their value—and firm proofs of success are hard to produce in education. The difficulties are multiplied ten-fold when teachers are expected to accept, not just a new technique for achieving the old ends, but methods that embody in themselves a new concept of the very purpose of education. That is why it is such a long and burdensome to convert a school system based primarily on memorisation into one involving understanding, active thinking, creativity what has come to be called 'problem solving'. Each step is not a step but a leap into the unknown, and the average teacher needs skilled and detailed help, and—what may seem to be a contradiction in terms—sympathetic goading if he is to make it at all. This is precisely the problem that we have to face and solve in the near future.

Very little systematic research has been undertaken on the diffusion of classroom practices even in the educationally advanced countries, and practically very rare in developing countries. The earlier researches of Paul Mort and his colleagues at Columbia University seemed to show that a period of 25 to 40 years was necessary in the United States, for anything like full diffusion of a new practice, but the rapid spread of such innovations as the PSSC Physics course (which started in 1957, and is now taken by a large number of the high school pupils studying physics in the United States) has shown that, under certain conditions, the period can be greatly reduced. This experience and some others of its type seem to indicate that the educational administrator can encourage and fasten the diffusion of new teaching practices in a number of ways. Some important of which are given hereunder.

1. Most of all the factors which render the system elastic enough for the outstanding teacher to break new ground will also make it easier for the average teachers to follow his example. However, mere permissiveness on the part of the authorities will not do the trick. They will need to play a more active part, with something that comes nearer to persuasion than to pressure but which still leaves no noubt in the teachers' minds that the Education Department and its officers favour certain changes. But it must be done with sensitivity and moderation, or the teachers will come

to regard the new methods as the Department's latest fad, and may try to apply them, with or without understanding, to the detriment of the normal work.

2. The main body of teachers will accept new methods more readily if the immediate goals set before them are limited ones. This means that the methods devised by the brilliant teacher or the subject specialist may have to be approached by stages, and that the stage demanded of each group of teachers may vary with their ability.
3. The usual devices for in-service training such as refresher courses, workshops, demonstrations, exhibitions of work, and visits of quite long duration (days, not hours) to see the new methods at work in pioneering schools should be adopted on a large scale. Used with discrimination and skill, films, tapes or radio can bring whole lessons to quite isolated schools, though not so much for their effect on the pupils as for their usefulness in providing a model of good teaching for the teachers.
4. It inerant instructors, specialised in certain subjects and class-levels of techniques, and working under the general direction of the District Education Officer, are even more vital at the stage of diffusing new methods than at the earlier stage of the first experiments.
5. Probably the quickest and most effective way of having new theories accepted is to embed them in the 'tools' of teaching—textbooks, teachers' guides, and teaching aids of all kinds. Some teaching of theory will, of course, still be essential. But it will *spring from* proposed practices instead of floating airily *above* them. The extent of the theory and the degree of detail with which the practices are set out will vary with the level of general education of the teachers. In the initial stages of development and with weaker schools, it

might be necessary for teacher's guides to go into a fair amount of detail on the series of lessons to be arranged throughout the school years, the methods to be used, the teaching aids to be prepared, the activities to be encouraged, and the tests and techniques of evaluation to be employed.

The technique referred to in the preceding paragraph may be described as the laying down of 'tramlines' on which the average teacher can move forward with confidence in his teaching. *This method is different from the traditional practice* under which the teacher is given lectures on general principles and is then expected to apply them with no more aid than is given by a mediocre textbook that ofted clashes with the very principles that are being advocated. It is, of course, the administrator's responsibility to ensure that, while providing 'tram-lines' for the mass of the teachers, there is still enough freedom left for the bold few to travel more freely. But with this pre-caution, there is no doubt that these 'tramlines' of progress *are* the techniques that will be particularly effective for diffusing new methods.

It is obvious that this laying down of tramlines is not a 'once and for all time' business —it requires continuous renewal. When an administrator lays down a set of tramlines with immense effort (it takes some years to do so), he generally finds that his 'progressive' tramlines have become a new 'orthodoxy' and that he will have to start laying them down once again and that there will be the same old resistance for breaking away from the earlier tramlines. But that is an inevitable and perennail problem that every educational reformer must face. The provisions made to enable the outstanding teachers to leave the tramlines will help the rest also to leave them in course of time, while the more adventurous teachers will go still further a head to fresh fields and pastures new.

It will be seen that the essence of our recommendation is that only an elastic and dynamic system of education can provide the needed conditions to encourage initiative, experimentation and creativity among teachers and thereby lay the foundations of educational progress. We firmly believe that the risks of freedom and trust in teachers that are implied in this approach are not greater than those of undue restriction and distrust and they are more worth taking. We should learn to delegate authority, to trust our teachers, to encourage the capacity for leadership amongst them, to treat every institution as having a personality of its own which it should try to develop in an atmosphere of freedom. This would need dynamic leadership at all levels, determined to give education a new deal and to make every teacher, educational officer and administrator put in the best of himself in this great cooperative endeavour.

## Teaching Materials and Textbooks, Teachers' Guides

The value of the textbooks as an effective tool of learning and of diffusion of improved teaching methods has been indicated in the preceding section. A good textbook, written by a qualified and competent specialist in the subject, and produced with due regard to quality of printing, illustrations and general get-up, stimulates the pupil's interest and helps the teacher considerably in his work. The provision of quality textbooks, and other teaching and learning materials, can thus be an effective programme for raising standards. The need to emphasise it is all the greater because it requires only a relatively small investment of resources. Moreover, a quality book need not cost appreciably more than the one that is indifferently produced.

### *Textbook's Quality*

Unfortunately, textbook writing and production have not received the attention they deserve. In most school subjects, there is a proliferation of low quality, sub-standard and badly produced books, particularly in the regional languages. This has been due to a number of factors among which mention may be made of

- the lack of interest shown by top-ranking scholars so that the writing of textbooks has been generally undertaken by persons whose abilities are far from equal to the task;
- the malpractices in the selection and prescription of text-books which defy control;
- the unscrupulous tactics adopted by several publishers;"
- the lack of research in the preparation and production of textbooks; and
- the almost total disregard by private publishers (who are interested only in profits) of the need to bring out ancillary books, such as teachers' guides to accompany textbooks.

### *Textbook's Production*

As education began to spread, the textbook industry became one of the very profitable fields for investment and the evils of the type mentioned above became more and more conspicuous. The attention of State Governments was soon drawn to them and it was decided that, in order to eliminate them, the State Governments should take over the production of textbooks. At present, most State Governments have adopted this policy and taken over the production of textbooks. The extent to which this responsibility has been assumed shows considerable variations—some States have produced only a few books at the primary stage while others have produced all books till the end of the secondary stage. In one or two States, not only production but even contribution and sale of textbooks have been taken over by the State.

There have been some definite gains from this policy. Private profiteering has disappeared and prices have been kept low. The malpractices and intrigues which used to be so common a feature of what used to be called the 'textbook racket' have also disappeared. The quality of books, has improved in several instances, although the general level of the books still remains poor and their standard does not often come up to that some of the well-established and efficient publishers. The main reason for this failure is that the Education Departments which have taken over the responsibility of textbook production have not adequately organised themselves for it. It is this weakness that is largely responsible for the shortcomings one often sees in the State-produced textbooks, *viz.* failure to revise books for long periods, misprints, poor production, failure to supply books in time, etc. We do not desire to underestimate these deficiencies. What we want to highlight are two points: the first is that these weaknesses do not lead to the conclusion, as, some interested parties are ever eager to show, that State-production of textbooks is wrong; and the second is to emphasise the urgency for the Education Departments to organise themselves properly for this great educational responsibility they have undertaken.

State-production of textbooks, it must be noted, is only one step in the direction of improving the quality of textbooks. But by itself, it can achieve little and if adequate steps are not taken in time to organise the activity on right lines, it may even put the clock back. We, therefore, recommend that emphasis should be placed on developing the programme of textbook production on right lines. Some concrete suggestions from this prom of view are made in the paragraphs that follow.

### *National Level Programme*

It is essentiat that the best talent available in the country should be brought together to produce the textbooks and other literature needed, both at the school and at the university stages. This can only be done at the national level by agencies set up by the Government of India.

1. For the university stage, the Ministry of Education is bringing out a series of low-priced and subsidised books in collaboration with appropriate authorities in the USA, the USSR and the UK. This is a useful scheme and its significance has now become even greater. It should be expanded and vigorously developed, along with schemes for books written by Indian authors. We lay great emphasis on the latter schemes. We recommend that as a matter of national policy, nearly all books at the undergraduate state, including those for professional subjects, should be written by Indian authors. In the preparation of these books, fullest use should, of course, be made of foreign sources. This goal should be capable of realisation within 5 to 10 years.
2. At the school stage, we welcome the steps taken by the NCERT to produce textbooks with the help of scholars available in the country. Some books have already come out; and more will come out soon. These books are meant for use by State Governments who can use them with or without changes. We hope that the State Governments will make full use of this pioneer venture to improve the quality of their books.
3. The production of textbooks and allied materials at the national level will be greatly facilitated if the Government of India were to establish, in the public sector, an autonomous organisation, functioning on commercial lines, for the production of textbooks. We have recommended the establishment of similar organisations at the State level also. But there will be a large number of books, especially in the scientific

and technical sector, which can only be produced on a national basis. It would also be desirable to produce several other categories of books at the national level, either for reducing cost or for improving quality or for purposes of national integration. We, therefore, feel that in organisation of this type at the national level is urgently needed. We recommend that the Ministry of Education should set up a small committee to work out the details of this project and take ail the necessary steps to bring it into existence as early as possible.

Textbooks produced at the national level will have other advantages as well. One of our major recommendations is that we should make an attempt to evolve national standards at the end of the primary, lower secondary and the higher secondary stages. The definition of these standards as well as the organisation of a programme for their practical implementation will be greatly facilitated by the production of textbooks at the national level. Such books can indicate the expected standard of attainment far more precisely than any curricula or syllabi; and their practical use in schools is the surest method to raise standards and make the teaching in schools in the different parts of the country fairly comparable. In a subject like mathematics or science, for instance, there is not much scope for local variations and the adoption of common textbooks in all parts of the country is not only feasible, but also desirable from several points of view. The same can be said about a common textbook in citizenship prepared from the point of view of national integration and used in all schools of the country. History is another difficult subject to teach, especially from the point of view of social and national integration; and authoritative well-written books on the subject can be of immense help to all teachers. At present, there is hardly any common book which all the students in India read; and that is one of the reasons why our educational system contributes so little to national integration. On the other hand, if we had, say, a set of 100 books on different topics written by the best of our scholars which would be translated and be available in *every* school and *if* an average student were expected to read them in his school course as a matter of routine, the entire thinking of the rising generation would be different and national integration could be immensely strengthened.

### *State Level Programme*

While attempts to improve textbooks at the national level are thus welcome, they cannot be the sole attempts for this crucial reform. Their most effective service is to stimulate other centres into activity and especially to promote similar enterprise at State levels. We recommend that each State should organise an adequately manned expert sections for the production of textbooks for schools. They should make as much use of the work done at the national level as possible. But there is no escape from the fact that each State will have to produce several textbooks in areas where national books will net be available. Even in areas where national books are available, independent attempts by the States will stimulate each other and the Centre itself.

We can hope for the best results only when the national and all the State centres for textbook production are functioning actively and in close collaboration.

The following points should be kept in view by the State Education Departments in organising their programmes of textbook production:

1. A separate agency, preferably functioning on an autonomous and commercial basis, should be set up, in close liason with the Education Department for the production of textbooks and teaching aids. It would be extremely difficult, if not impossible, to have within

the four walls of usual departmental procedures, the autonomy and freedom which such an undertaking essentially needs.

2. Production of textbooks is a continuous process. For instance, it takes a year or even more to produce a textbook and a further year for try-out and revision. Within a year of its adoption on a large scale, a process of evaluation has to start; and very soon thereafter, it will be discovered that it needs revision. The machinery set up, therefore, should be adequate to follow all these steps for *every* textbook. It should be an objective of policy to see that a textbook is continuously revised and kept up to date and that a thorough revision takes place at least once in five years, if not oftener. The need for frequent revisions of textbooks is obvious, even if the curricula were to remain unchanged. But we do visualise, as stated in the last chapter, a continual deepening of the curricula. In fact, very often a revision of textbooks will be necessitated, not by a revision of curricula, but as a means of changing and deepening them.
3. No useful purpose is served by having only one textbook in a subject for a given class—this is almost invariably the position under the existing programmes of nationalisation. It should be an important objective of policy to have at least three or four books in each subject for each class and leave it open to the teachers to choose the book best suited to the school. This is necessary even if there were to be a common syllabus for all the schools. We have recommended, however, that there should be more than one approved syllabus and that each school should be permitted to adopt the syllabus best suited to its own conditions. In such a case, a multiple choice of books should be available for each syllabus.

4. When Government gets books written, the payment to authors is often so niggardly that the ablest scholars are not generally attracted. This is the one point where private enterprise often scores over State-produced textbooks. It is, therefore, necessary to adopt liberal policies for remuneration, comparable to those of the private trade, and to attract the best people to write books.
5. State-production of textbooks is not to be used for purposes of earning profits; its sole purpose is to produce the best books and to make them available to the children at the lowest cost. The entire organisation should, therefore, be run on a no-profit and no-less basis. The sales of State-produced books, however, are so large and certain, that even when no profits as such is charged and the price is merely rounded off to the nearest five paise, large margins are left over and these are enough to cover the costs of research, overhead establishment and the preparation of ancillary aids like teachers' guides.
6. The incentive to write books should be encouraged in as many quarters as possible. Apart from commissioning selected persons write textbooks, which wilt have to be done in many cases, the Departments should also invite manuscripts, proposals, etc., and be ever on the hunt for new talent. There should be high level committees of professional persons to judge books or proposals submitted; and approved books should be adopted by the Departments and published after making suitable arrangements with the authors.
7. Special encouragements should be given to teachers to write textbooks. In the USSR, even the highest positions in universities can be obtained by writing outstanding textbooks. Our universities can follow this example. We also suggest that learned societies

should give adequate professional recognition to outstanding textbooks.

8. Good textbooks 'are not enough; they should be supplemented by teachers' guides and other instructional material. A teachers' guide, as we have mentioned above, should give detailed assistance to teachers. Even for graduate teachers in the United States, some of the new courses being evolved in mathematics, science and social studies contain a great deal of detailed suggestions. The poorly educated and insecure teacher tends to drop into a dreary routine in which every lesson is taught in the same way, and he needs quite detailed suggestions on a variety of methods, which can make his teaching more lively and effective. It is only with the help of such detailed framework of support and guidance that a large number of teachers, particularly in the primary schools, will get off the beaten track.

There are really three aspects to the textbook production programme: (a) *Production aspect* which includes all matters relating to printing and publication; (b) *Academic* aspect which includes the preparation of textbooks, try-out and evaluation; and (c) *Distribution* aspect which includes storage, sales, etc.

The first is the most important, aspects, and the responsibility for it will have to be squarely accepted by the State-Education Departments on the lines we have recommended above. The second is discretionary. We find that some State Governments have accepted direct responsibility for it and established separate text book presses. This is the direction in" which we should move. The third is really self-continued and is not inseparably linked with the first two. In one State where the State Government had assumed direct responsibility for distribution of textbooks, we found that the precious time of a number of field officers was taken up by sales, accounts and stock-keeping. We recommend that this activity should be promoted through student cooperatives which every educational institution (or group of educational institutions) should be encouraged to establish, and that it should not be assumed directly by the Education Departments.

*Provision of Essential Teaching Aids.* In assessing the needs of the teacher from the point of view of teaching methods, one is forced to admit that in the majority of schools, particularly at the primary stage, there is still an almost total absence of basic equipment and teaching aids—a good blackboard, a small library, essential maps and charts, simple science apparatus, and necessary display materials. The supply of such basic equipment and teaching aids to every school in the country is essential for the improvement of the quality of teaching. It would indeed bring about an educational revolution, in the country. We recommend that lists of minimum-teaching aids and equipment needed by each category of schools should be prepared. These may be kept as economical and frugal as possible. But once a certain minimum equipment is considered necessary, steps should be taken to see that it is given to every school on a high priority basis. As in Madras State, the help of the local community could be harnessed in developing this programme. As a first step, we recommend that a good blackboard should be immediately given to all schools.

Several suggestions were made to us to the effect that we should adopt new techniques of teaching which are now coming into use in the advanced countries. These technique involve the large-scale use of films, radios, tape-recorders and other audio-visual, aids, the introduction of open and closed circuit television, and the provision of language laboratories, programmed instructional methods and simple and highly-sophisticated forms of teaching machines. With regard to the use of films,, filmstrips and other simple audio-visual equipment, it may be possible to make these teaching aids available to every school complex (and through it to every school even in rural areas). In this connection, we invite attention to the Report of a Study Group on Classroom-Science Films (their recommendations apply to the teaching of other subjects also) with which we broadly agree. In addition, it should also be possible to equip the majority of upper primary and secondary schools with low cost radio-sets. We recommend that Education Departments should work with the All India Radio for the use of radio lessons, supplemented with printed material for the teachers, and, if possible, for the pupils. We also recommend the broadcasting of special radio talks, in the early morning or late evening, specially designed for teachers which will help to deepen their subject knowledge and guide them in lesson preparation. The more sophisticated forms of the newer techniques, however, can be used, generally speaking as, this stage of our educational development only on an experimental basis and in a few schools. It has to be remembered that schools cannot use an equipment which is much beyond the level of technology in the society. Sophisticated equipment given to rural schools, for instance, cannot be maintained and soon falls into disrepair. A few progressive schools may be equipped with new aids like language laboratories and programmed instructional material; but such techniques may preferably be tried out, in the first instance, in the education and training of teachers. The majority of teachers in our schools will have to rely on inexpensive teaching equipment which are easily available in the locality or are made by them with proper encouragement and little financial assistance. The programmes that will help us most, in the immediate future, in improving the teaching in our schools are, therefore, the following:

1. The training of teachers in the use and preparation of simple and improvised teaching aids;

2. The use of the school workshop—and also of programmes of work-experience—to prepare the teaching aids required by the school itself and by other schools in the neighbourhood;
3. Manufacture of simple equipment on a large scale for reducing cost, and its distribution to schools; and
4. Sharing the more costly equipment in common by schools in a given neighbourhood. For instance, a group of schools in the neighbourhood may have a projector in common. A good laboratory in one school can be used, according to a carefully prepared plan, by other schools nearby. A group of schools may have a circulating library, and so on.

### *Size of Class*

It will be generally agreed that there cannot be a marked improvement in methods of teaching if the teacher is required to teach very large classes as a matter of routine. The phenomenal expansion of primary and secondary education in recent years has resulted in overcrowding in schools, especially in urban areas, where accommodation is not easily available for the extension of the school building or the opening of new sections. The class size sometimes grows to abnormal proportions. A class of sixty children is a common sight in a city. We ourselves have seen, in the course of our tour, classes of sixty and even sixty-five children in a few secondary schools. Quite often, the classroom is not able to accommodate easily such a large number. The problem is solved by pushing the teacher's chair—there is no place for a teachers' desk—into a corner and bringing the front benches almost up to the black-board! In conditions like these all talk of creative teaching ceases to have any significance.

*Present Position.* The size of classes at different school stages, on the basis of information supplied by the State

Governments for 25 districts selected from eight States in a special study carried out by the Commission.

We find that 11.1 per cent of the teachers at the lower primary stage teach classes of 50-59, 6.5 per cent take classes of 60-69 pupils, and 14.3 per cent have to deal with classes of 70 pupils and more. Some of these classes will be, of course, in single-teacher schools, where one teacher has to take two, three and sometimes even five combined classes." Similarly, at the higher primary and the secondary stages, the position is not much better. The percentage of teachers handling classes of 50 to 70 pupils and above is 13.2 in class VI, 10.2 in class VII, 19.3 in class VIII, 24.1 in class IX, 19.8 in class X, 29.5 in class XI and 36.7 in class XII. It will be seen that the number of teachers handling such large class increases as we go up the educational ladder.

*Difficulties of Teaching Large Classes.* Methods of teaching in classes of fifty pupils and more cannot be satisfactory. However capable a teacher may be, he cannot pay individual attention to a large number of children, give special assistance to the weaker ones, guide the brighter ones to proceed at a faster pace in an attempt to help one and all to reach the maximum of their capacities. In these circumstances the average teacher will be tempted to resort to rote memorisation. Assignments given will generally not be checked and composition exercises will be marked during periods of spasmodic energy. The poor quality of teaching in the ordinary secondary school in urban areas may partly be attributed to overcrowded classrooms.

We do not, however, support those educational theorists who contend that a class should not have more than twenty or twenty-five pupils. It would be extremely unrealistic for our teachers to think in terms of this ideal. There is indeed no such thing as an ideal class size, and there is no sanctity about the number twenty-five or twenty. In our country, classes of a somewhat larger size than what may be strictly considered as desirable cannot be avoided for a long time to come. Some of the educationally advanced countries are also facing a similar problem. Teachers, should reconcile themselves to the acceptance of this inescapable necessity. It is also the responsibility of the training institutions to have a more practical approach to the problem and to evolve methods which would help the teachers to teach classes of this size without a complete abandonment of all pedagogic principles.

The class size in classes I and II has a special significance. More than half the enrolment at the primary stage is in these to classes; and very often, they are large classes of 60 or more. In such cases, our first recommendation would be that the requisite number of teachers should be provided and the class size reduced as indicated above. But if this were not possible we would Prefer to break this class into two classes of about 30-35 students and engage them only for three hours a day and request the teacher to engage two such classes per day. This would be a far better method of education than the present system of herding 70 or so pupils in one class and keeping them there for six hours a day.

*Multiple-Class Teaching.* About 40 per cent of our schools are single-teacher schools and even in other schools, the proportion of big schools where one teacher teaches one class is very small. More than half of our teachers, therefore, have to teach more than one class at a time.

In a situation of this type, research in multiple-class teaching is badly needed; and training institutions have to make a special effort in orientating teachers to the special techniques that have to be used under such conditions.

## School Buildings

The provision of school buildings is extremely unsatisfactory at present. At the primary stage, only about 30 per cent of the schools are stated to have been housed in satisfactory buildings. The corresponding proportion at the secondary stage is stated to be about 50. This shows the great backlog of unconstructed school buildings which has to be cleared during the next few years. In addition, buildings; will have to be provided for the additional enrolment which will rise with increasing speed. The problem, therefore, has three aspects:

1. provision of the necessary funds;
2. reduction of the building costs to the minimum level possible; and
3. the devising of a suitable machinery which can implement the programme expeditiously and economically.

### *Funds for School Building*

We recommend that the allocations for construction of school buildings in the Central and State budgets should be increased. This is one area where the local community can make a significant contribution. Schemes of grant-in-aid should, therefore, be devised under which assistance from the State will be available to local communities, on a basis of equalisation, for the construction of school buildings. Wherever possible, loan programmes for the construction of buildings should be encouraged. Grant in-aid and loans should also be available to private schools, on a fairly liberal basis, for building construction.

### *Reduction of Costs*

A number of committees have examined this question for both the Central and State Governments, on behalf of the Ministry of Education, the Ministry of Works and the Planning Commission. In addition, the UGC has prepared detailed norms for hostels, staff quarters, libraries, etc., and the Central

Building Research Institute at Roorkee and the Indian Standards Institute have made recommendations in this area. The result of all these is that there exist, for most types of school and colleges, space and planning norms and type plans and a good deal of sound advice that can help in reducing costs. What is required now is a mechanism that will put this information into practice.

In view of the acute shortage of traditional classical building materials and the shortage of accommodation, many schools are today operating in what are classified as temporary constructions by the PWD and some even in thatched huts. We find that there is a strong prejudice against such structures. In our view this prejudice against the use of 'temporary' buildings or thatched huts for school purposes is totally unjustified. Designed and constructed with a raised floor and high doors and windows with plenty of ventilation, these structures serve more than adequately as school buildings. This should not, however, be misunderstood to imply that *kacha* buildings are always better. This is not so; and some *kacha* buildings prove costlier in the long run because of heavier costs of maintenance. What we wish to emphasize is the need to accept well-planned *kacha* structures as part of our system and to highlight simplicity and utility rather than ostentation in the construction of buildings.

### *Buildings in Rural Areas*

The problem of school buildings needs to be discussed separately for urban and rural areas. In the former case, land values are high; and very often enough land is not available at all. Sophisticated structures are, therefore, necessary, even in order to keep in tune with the immediate environment. In the rural areas on the other hand, land is cheap and readily available; and sophisticated structures often look grotesque in a village atmosphere.

We recommend that everything should be done to encourage local initiative and local contribution, in cash, kind or labour for the erection of the schools. A special device that can be of great use is that government should supply only the framework—which can be prefabricated—and the local people should be expected to raise the plinth and fill up the walls. The 'nucleus' approach recommended by the Ministry of Education will be of great help and deserves to be generally adopted.

***Buildings in Urban Areas***

In urban areas, the following steps should be taken for achieving economy in the construction of educational buildings:

1. *Judicious Selection of Specifications and Local Materials.* The existing practice of playing safe by adopting conventional specifications is not conducive to economical construction. Economy can be achieved through the selection of locally available materials, use of cheaper materials, omission altogether of certain finishes and acceptance of a lower standard of constriction. In all these steps, the governing factors would, however, be the availability of materials, climatic conditions, safety of buildings and recurring costs on maintenance.

2. *Techniques of Construction.* With careful planning and designing, even the so-called 'temporary' structures can be made to serve a better purpose than many of the rented buildings in which schools are often housed. Such structures should be built, wherever climatic and other conditions permit. If pucka buildings are absolutely necessary, an increasing reliance is needed on the improved techniques of construction such as the use of framed structures, cavity walls, prefabricated components, RCC framed for doors and windows

and components evolved by the Central Building Research Institute and other research organisations.

### *Expeditious Construction*

In order to expedite the constriction of school buildings, the following steps are recommended:

1. *Rural Areas.* In rural areas, there are no local contractors available. Contractors from urban areas generally charge higher rates when they are required to work in villages. The departmental machinery is also not adequate to reach most of the outlying villages. For the construction of village school buildings, therefore, we recommend that the agency of the local communities or village panchayats should be utilised to the fullest extent possible.
2. *Urban Areas.* In urban areas, we recommend that the local agencies like municipalities and corporations should be utilised fully for construction of school buildings. They have the necessary technical staff and can also contribute towards the cost of such buildings. If the responsibility for providing buildings for local schools is placed on municipalities and if a suitable system of grant-in-aid is devised, the progress in this sector would be accelerated.

### *Supervision and Standardisation of School Buildings*

For construction of government school buildings, to assist the voluntary organisations for the purpose, to supervise the general programme of construction of school buildings in a State, and to continually introduce improved and economic techniques, we recommend the adoption of the following additional measures:

1. *Formation of Educational Building Development Groups.* Each State should have an Educational Building

Development Group, within the Public Works Department but working in close association with the Education Department, and consisting of an architect, an educationist, an administrator, a civil engineer and a cost accountant, all working on a full time basis (with power to co-opt representatives of special technical skills). The main function of the group would be to improve the planning and construction of government school buildings but its advice should be available for private schools also. There should also be a Building Development Group working at the Centre, for effectively coordinating the working of State-level Groups.

The other functions of the Groups will be (a) to study building requirements in the light of new teaching techniques, (b) to develop in cooperation with manufacturers new building techniques and specifications, (c) to evolve functional and economic type plans for various types of educational buildings, (d) to arrive at a correct assessment of costs of materials and labour required, (e) to conduct field trials, (f) to evaluate the plans, specifications and building techniques already in use, and (g) to study methods of maximising the use of indigenous materiels. The Group at the Centre could profitably bring out a journal highlighting the latest techniques of construction, and researches at home and abroad on conventional buildings.

The State Government should ensure that the recommendations of these Development Groups are followed.

1. To avoid delays in the construction of government buildings a separate unit of PWD should be set up for execution of educational buildings programmes.
2. When the Groups in the different States are well established, the possibility of making them function within a rigid framework of maximum cost per place

and minimum standards' as is being successfully done in the United Kingdom, should be explored.

3. *Formation of Educational Building Consortia.* After the Educational Building Development Groups have standardised the plans and the technique of construction, the possibility should be examined of establishing Education Building Consortia (on the lines of similar associations, popularly knows as CLASP, in the UK) to exploit fully the advantages of industrialised buildings.
4. *Buildings for Private Schools.* The economy measures worked out by the Educational Building Development Group in each State for reducing the cost of educational buildings should be made known to the managements of private educational institutions in the State, and the grant-in-aid given to a private management for a buildings should be subject to the upper cost limits worked out.
5. *Standardisation.* Layouts, dimensions, specifications and methods of construction for any particular region should be standardised by the Educational Buildings Development Group mentioned above so that mass production of the different components on a factory scale can be undertaken resulting in economy as well as speed of construction. Considerable work in the field of standardisation has been done by organizations like the Indian Standards Institute which could serve as a basis for further studies.

**School Health Services**

The provision of school health services (including school meals) is of great importance. The problem has recently been studied by the School Health Committee under the chairmanship of Shrimati Renuka Ray. We broadly agree with the recommendations of the Committee.

## Counselling and Guidance

### *Guidance Services: Aim and Scope*

Guidance services have a much wider scope and function than merely that of assisting students in making educational and vocational choices. The aims of guidance are both adjustive and developmental: it helps the student in making the best possible adjustment to the situations in the educational institution and in the home and at the same time facilities the development of all aspects of his personality. Guidance, therefore, should psychological or social service which is peripheral to educational purposes. It is meant for all students, not just for those who deviate from the norm in one direction or the other. It is also a continuous process aimed at assisting the individual to make decisions and adjustments from time to time.

### *Primary Education Guidance*

Guidance should begin from the lowest class of the primary school. It can be used in helping pupils to make a satisfactory transition from home to school; in diagnosing difficulties in the learning of basic educational skills; in identifying pupils in need of special education (e.g., the gifted, the backward, the physically handicapped); in helping potential drop-outs to stay in school; in guiding pupils to develop insight into the world of work and favourable attitudes towards work; and in assisting in plans for their further education or training. Little has been done so far in the shape of guidance services at the primary stage because of the large numbers of institutions involved, the poor qualifications of the teachers and the absence of resources. It would, therefore, be unrealistic for a long time to come to think of providing qualified counsellors in these schools. Some guidance functions can, however, be performed by well-trained primary school teachers. Community resources can also be mobilised to meet some of the guidance needs of the young pupils.

Suggestions for making a beginning in guidance in the primary school are outlined below:

1. There should be at least one lecturer in the training school who should be able to deal with the subject of principles of guidance and mental hygiene.
2. The training programme for primary school teachers should include familiarisation with simple diagnostic testing, and with the problem of individual differences and their implications for classroom practices.
3. Guidance services should be introduced in the training institutions and in schools attached to the institutions so that the trainees may get first-hand knowledge of the problems involved in their organisation.
4. Simple literature for the occupational orientation of children may be prepared and made available in the regional languages.
5. Wherever possible, short in-service courses in guidance should be provided for primary school teachers.
6. At the end of the primary stage, children and parents should be helped in the selection of courses for further education, and the selection should not be based on the examination results alone.

***Secondary Education Guidance***

One of the main functions of guidance at the secondary level is to aid in the identification and development of the abilities and interests of adolescent pupils. It helps these pupils to understand their own strengths and limitations and to do scholastic work at the level of their ability to gain information about educational and vocational opportunities and requirements, to make realistic educational and vocational choices and plans based on a consideration of all relevant factors; and to find solutions to their problems of personal and social adjustment the school and the home, Guidance services also help headmasters and teachers to understand their students as individuals and to create situations in which the students can learn more effectively.

Following the recommendations of the Secondary Education Commission, the Ministry of Education set up a Central Bureau of Educational and Vocational Guidance in 1954 to give technical advice and help to the nascent guidance movement in the field of secondary education. Guidance became a Centrally sponsored scheme in the Third Plan and 13 Bureaus have now been set up for the development of guidance services in the States. These Central and State-level organisations have developed a modest programme of guidance, and services are rendered to the pupils in the schools by trained counsellors and career masters with the help of the teachers. By the end of the third plan, the number of schools offering some kind of guidance was about 3,000, which constituted only about 13 per cent of the total number of secondary schools in the country. Again the majority of these 3,000 schools have only a career master on the staff and offer only an information service. Very few institutions have a full time or part-time counsellor for giving effective guidance help, including testing and counselling.

It is thus clear that although there is an organised movement for providing guidance services in the country, the progress made has been very slow. The ultimate objective should of course be to introduce adequate guidance services in all secondary schools, with a trained counsellor in charge of the programme. Since, however, neither financial allocations nor training facilities for guidance will be available on such a large scale, it is necessary that a short-range programme should be adopted for the next 20 years. We, therefore, make the following recommendations:

1. A minimum guidance service should be made available to all secondary schools by having one Visiting School

Counsellor for every ten schools located within a reasonable distance of one another, and by allocating the simpler guidance functions to the teachers.

2. At the same time, in order to demonstrate what a really comprehensive guidance service is like and what it can achieve, it would be desirable to set up comprehensive guidance services in a few carefully selected schools, preferably one in each district.
3. The necessary supervisory staff to inspect and offer consultation to the school 'workers should be appointed in the State Bureaux of Guidance.

We believe it is necessary that all secondary school teachers should be given some understanding of guidance concepts and simple guidance techniques as a part of the programme intended for every trainee. Special or advanced courses should be provided for those who wish to study the subject in depth. Every training college should have on its staff a person having at least the training considered essential for school counsellors. Provision should also exist for the in-service training of the training college staff in guidance and counselling.

Adequate arrangements should be made for the professional training of guidance workers. The training of career masters may be undertaken by the State Bureaux as well as the training colleges with the collaboration of the vocational guidance officers of the National Employment Service. Professional courses of longer duration should be offered by the universities. Until such courses are started, it may be necessary for the older State Bureaux which have been offering this programme to continue to do so. As the number of persons capable of conducting training programmes for guidance workers is extremely limited, higher level training programmes in guidance to prepare qualified guidance workers to undertake training and research should be initiated at the national level.

### General Proposals

(a) Programmes for the development of guidance literature, occupational information materials, films and filmstrips, and psychological tests, need to be accelerated, care being given to avoid duplication of effort through increased communication among agencies working in these fields. Coordination of efforts should characterise all guidance programmes.

(b) Schools should be assisted in providing hobbies and recreational activities as well as part-time employment opportunities for their students. These should be organised in such a manner as to provide meaningful experiences for the students, and enable them to explore and develop their interests and abilities.

(c) In addition to the training and extension programmes in guidance mentioned earlier, emphasis should be laid on research pertaining to guidance in the Indian situation.

### Search for and Development of Talent

*Significance:* A dearth of competent and trained manpower is now felt in nearly every branch of national life, and is probably one of the biggest bottlenecks to progress. Poor as we are financially, the poverty of trained intellect is still greater. We might do well to remember Whitehead's warning: 'In the modern would the rule is absolute—any race which, does not value trained intelligence is doomed'.

*Present Position:* Native intelligence is generally distributed equitably throughout the population. If it is duly discovered and developed, our large population can be our most valuable asset. Unfortunately, very little of the available talent is now discovered and developed, due to several adverse factors :

(a) Even the talent that enters school and succeeds in climbing the educational ladder does not flower fully because it is not discovered sufficiently early and is often studying in poor schools. For obtaining the best results in quality, talent has to be located early and allowed to grow in the best atmosphere and under the best teachers.

(b) In a large majority of the homes, the environment is deprivatory on account of the illiteracy of the parents and poverty, and does not allow the available native talent to develop itself fully.

(c) we still try to determine talent by considering total marks obtained in an examination. This is a very in effective method. The highly gifted students are far too" creative to be confined within the perimeters of classroom instruction, textbooks and examinations. The genius in one field is generally poor in several others and in our examination system, a genius is more likely to fail or put up only a mediocre 'total' of marks than to come out at the top: Ramanujam and Tagore could not even pass the routine examinations where mediocrities shone. We should, therefore, search separately for each especial talent, whether in mathematics, science, literature fine arts, sports or technology.

(d) A good deal of potential talent never enters school. At the primary stage, the proportion of children not enrolled' varies from 10 to 60 per cent in different areas. Even, among those who enter, about 40 per cent are eliminated in class I itself and only about 25 per cent belonging to about the top 20 per cent of families in the society, complete primary education. Secondary education is largely a privilege of the top 10 per cent of the families and higher education of the 5 per cent.

It is not an easy thing to identify gifted students, except perhaps m mathematics and, to some extent, in science Sustained and energetic research is needed. But as talent is the most valuable asset a country can have, the returns will be immense. Moreover, the search for talent must be a continuous process and has to be taken up at all stage. The secondary stage, however is the most crucial;,and a reference has already been made to the manner in which universities can help in the identification of gifted students at this stage and help them to develop.

*Recommendations:* Elsewhere, we have made several proposals which will assist in this programme for the discovery and development of talent. The provision of five years of good and effective primary education to every child will enable the country to cast its net for talent to the widest extent possible. The large programme of scholarships proposed at all stages will ensure that all gifted students, or at least the top 5 toll per cent of the relevant age-group, will be enabled to receive the highest education possible. The placement programme which we suggest will also make it possible for them to study in the best institutions available at each stage.

In addition to these programmes, it is also necessary to introduce enrichment programmes for the brighter students in as many schools as possible and ultimately in every school. The performance of talented students in the enrichment programmes should be recorded in special certificates which will indicate to the colleges or other institutions of higher education their special abilities and attainments. Care should be taken to ensure that the enrichment programmes do not degenerate into coaching for passing examinations with higher marks. The flexibility in the school curriculum that we have proposed in the preceding chapter would enable the schools to provide enriched or advanced courses for the talented and help them to progress at their own speed. This will also release time for teachers to help the average and backward students.

A variety of extra-mural programmes can also be organised for the talented students, either separately by each school or by schools acting in cooperation or by the Education Departments. For instance:

1. Well-planned visits may be arranged to laboratories, museums, and other places.
2. Talented students may be brought into contact with persons engaged in the types of work for which the students show special ability or interest. These persons may be able to provide occasional opportunities for the students to work in their special fields.
3. Hostels or Day Centres may be made available for those students whose home environment is not conducive to proper study.
4. A five to six-week summer vacation programme can be arranged for a group of academically talented children from different schools, brought together to an educational centre having special facilities of staff, library, laboratory and equipment. The programme may be renewed for the particular group from year to year, so that the students get an opportunity to develop their special talent over a number of years.

In planning for the development of the talented student, it should be remembered that it is not only his intellectual competence or special ability that needs to be developed. The development of the emotional and social aspects of his personality, and of socially desirable attitudes, is also very important.

### *Role of Counsellor*

The role of the counsellor in the promotion of talent can

be very important. The counsellor with his detailed knowledge of each talented student is in a unique position to formulate a programme of enrichment for him and to suggest the necessary modifications in the curricular and extra-curricular requirements. Where special counsellors are not available, this task will fall on the teachers. It will, therefore, be necessary to train teachers for this responsibility through in-service seminars and special courses. It should be impressed on them that the classroom atmosphere and the attitudes of teachers is of considerable importance. In a social and educational set-up like ours where the relationship between the teacher and the taught is still largely authoritarian, the general tendency is to suppress any urges and interests that deviate from the classroom. Therefore, the first requirement for the promotion of talent, is for the teachers to create an atmosphere of free expression in the classroom and to provide opportunities for creative work amply.

## Educating Backward Child

With the fast expansion of educational facilities, the number of backward children in schools is also increasing. Many of them drop out of schools at one stage or another, either because of their inability to satisfy the academic standards or the boredom and frustration they feel in the pursuit of an academic programme which is largely unrelated to their needs and interests. Quite a few of these children manage to enter high school or even college with their very poor performance.

*Types of Backwardness:* Backwardness is largely due to one of two reasons which sometimes overlap : (1) mental handicap or low intelligence, arising from hereditary or congenital factors or disease or injury; (2) under-achievement or inability to perform up to the level of one's intelligence, especially in persons intellectually well endowed, frequently due to emotional conflict, lack of motivation, poor study habits, cultural deprivation and economic handicaps. On the basis of studies made in educationally advanced countries, it is estimated that seventy-five per cent of the backward children belong to the first category, usually referred to as the mentally charged, and the remaining twenty-five per cent belong to the second category, usually designated as the under-achievers. In the present case, the latter category would be obviously much greater. Both these categories of students, for different reasons, are unable to profit from normal education. The result is a wastage of educational facilities and of human resources, which a developing country can afford hardly.

*Meeting the Needs of Slow Learners:* The mentally handicapped are generally classified into four groups: the idiots; the imbeciles; the educable mentally handicapped morons; and the dull or slow-learners. The first three groups of backward children, who have an intelligence quotient below 75, cannot benefit from formal education in ordinary classes. Suitable provision should, however, be made for the education of the dull, who on account of their slower rate of mental development, cannot learn at the ordinary pace of normal children. In the ordinary classes, where instruction is traditionally geared to the needs of the average child, the dull have to work under a great hardship. They need individual attention, special remedial help and probably also a modified curriculum to suit their rate of learning. In big cities, it may be possible to establish special schools for them as has been done in some educationally advanced countries, but in most cases, special classes in the ordinary schools and individual tuition to the extent possible are the only general remedy. Such a treatment is likely to be better for their proper emotional and social development also.

*Problem of the Under-achievers:* The group of under-achievers consists of children who are not intellectually dull, but are at least of average and may even be of superior ability. The failure of such children should be of great concern to a developing country like ours, which cannot remain indifferent to this loss of potential manpower within the higher ability range. Several factors—physical, intellectual, emotional and environmental—contribute to the failure of the under-achiever to come up to the level of his latent abilities. The first step is to diagnose the causes of this failure by observation, interrogation and the application of psychological tests, if possible. Such a collation of data will make it possible to have a total appraisal of the situation and indicate lines of remedial treatment.

Once the child's errors and difficulties are located, a remedial programme should be formulated and carried out. The remedial programme should aim at correcting the basic errors, raising his attainment level in the subject or subjects, re-establishing his confidence in himself and in his ability to succeed, and creating for him new interest and motivation in his studies. The remedial measures should involve the student himself as much as possible and should be organised individually or in small groups. The assessment of the student's progress should be made not against any external standards but with reference to his own previous performance. Remedial programmes are particularly needed in reading, spelling and number work in the earlier stages, and in language and computational skills in the later stages.

Since these educationally retarded children are not under-achieving because of innate low mental capacity, their needs can be met by remedial arrangements within the school system. What the student requires is help for a limited period and within a limited area of study. This may be done by assigning the responsibility to one or two interested teachers during specific periods in the week. Where child guidance clinics exist —and this is a very limited facility at present—the help of highly trained personnel will be available for a group of schools at regular intervals. Remedial groups could also be set up after school hours, two or three days in the week, with subject specialists in charge of each group.

Guidance and counselling services have an important role to play in the education of the backward, especially with regard to identification of the group, diagnosis of their special defects and planning for their education and future occupation. But these services have not been developed and the programme has to be carried on with whatever help and guidance can be given by teachers in the school. The essential factor for success of the programme is the coordinated approach that the entire school faculty should make to the problem of these children with a degree of sympathy and understanding and with an insight into child psychology born out of long experience. The teacher should ordinarily be able to give some help to the under-achievers. Parent-teacher associations should be mobilised for enlisting the cooperation of parents in dealing with special cases. It is necessary, however, that there should be at least one child guidance clinic in each major town, and it should be adequately staffed. Serious cases of backwardness should be referred to these clinics for diagnosis and remedial help.

### New Programme of Evaluation

The evils of the examination system in India are well known to everybody. The baneful effects of the system on education in general, and secondary education in particular, have been discussed in the reports of several committees and commissions. The Secondary Education Commission after reviewing these defects at the secondary education stage, recommended a new approach to school evaluation and made a number of concrete proposals, for the improvement of the external examination and the methods of internal assessment.

As a result of these proposals, a movement was started for examination reform, which gathered momentum with the establishment of the Central Examination Unit of trained evaluation officers by the Government of India in 1958. The outstanding feature of the new reform movement is the emphasis laid on the modern concept of evaluation which has found increasing acceptance in educational circles in India in recent years.

### *Evaluation: New Concept*

It is now agreed that evaluation is a continuous process, forms an integral part of the total system of education, and is intimately related to educational objectives. It exercises a great influence on the pupil's study habits and the teacher's methods of instruction and thus helps not only to measure educational achievement but also to improve it. The techniques of evaluation are means of collecting evidence about the student's development in desirable directions. These techniques should, therefore, be valid, reliable, objective and practicable. As the common method (and often the only method) of evaluation used at present in India is the written examination, a natural corollary of the acceptance of the new approach will be to improve the written examination in such a way that it becomes a valid and reliable measure of educational achievement. There are, however, several important aspects of the student's growth that cannot be measured by written examinations, and other methods such as observation techniques, oral tests and practical examinations, have to be devised for collecting evidence for the purpose. These methods need to be improved and made reliable instruments for assessing the student's performance and educational development.

### *Progress of the Movement for Reform*

During the seven years of its existence the Central Examination Unit has made a multipronged attack for the popularisation of new concept and techniques of evaluation.

It has worked with thousands of secondary school teachers in seminars and workshops, introduced hundreds of training college lecturers to the new techniques, established a very large pool of test items, trained paper-setters attached to different Boards of Secondary Education, published a good deal of literature on evaluation and carried out or sponsored several studies and investigations on various practical problems in examinations. As the work of the Unit expanded, the Government of India approved of the establishment of Evaluation Units in different States during the Third Plan period. So far, State Evaluation Units have started functioning in 12 States and one Union Territory.

But the task is a stupendous one, and it will take considerable time for the new measures to make their impact on objectives, learning experiences and evaluation procedures in school education. The improvements already made in the external examination by the different Boards have not removed all its major defects. The objectives have not yet been enlarged to include the testing of application and problem-solving abilities. The character of the school examinations, at least in the senior classes, is determined largely by that of the external examination, and the new techniques of evaluation are not readily adopted in these internal examinations. Moreover, all the efforts in the direction of reform have been confined to the field of secondary education. No attention has been paid to the improvement of examinations at the primary stage, and hardly any to the problems in this area at the university stage.

### *Lower Primary Stage Evaluation*

One of the main purposes of evaluation at the primary stage is to help the pupils to improve their achievement in the basic skills and to develop the right habits and attitudes with reference to the objectives of primary education. These objectives and their implications for evaluation should be made clear to the teachers. As has been suggested in an earlier chapter, it would be desirable to treat the lower primary stage covering classes I to IV as an ungraded unit, because this would help the children coming from different backgrounds to advance at their own pace. At the conditions in most primary schools, however, are not favourable to the general adoption of this procedure, we have recommended that the experiment should be tried out in the beginning in classes I and II, which should be regarded as a single ungraded unit. This will put an end to the existing practice of detentions in class I and the drop-outs and wastage resulting therefrom, and will also provide for continuity and flexibility in the educational programme of the first two classes. The two-year block may be divided into two groups, one for slow-learners and the other for fast-learners to enable different pupils to proceed at the level of their ability and move from one unit to another. Such a division, however, will be practicable only in a large-size school with more than one section in each class. If the experiment regarding the ungraded unit succeeds in classes I and II, it may be extended to the remaining classes of the lower primary stage. Teachers should be prepared for the ungraded system through the regular training courses and orientation programmes and should be helped with a supply of diagnostic tests and remedial material. The orientation may be given by the State Institutes of Education. Observation techniques, which are more reliable for assessing the pupil's growth at this stage than mere formal techniques, of evaluation, should be used by teachers in a planned and systematic manner.

### *High Primary State Evaluation*

At present evaluation in these classes is carried out largely by means of written examinations. We believe that due importance should be given here also to oral tests, which should form a part of the internal assessment. The teacher should be helped in such assessment with a rich supply of evaluation materials prepared by the State Evaluation Organisations, including standardised achievement tests. Diagnostic testing is necessary here and indeed throughout the school stage. In most cases, such testing will be through simple teacher-made diagnostic tests. Cumulative record cards play a vital role in indicating the growth and development of the pupil at each stage, his academic and emotional problems, and his difficulties of adjustment, if any, and the directions in which remedial action is to be taken to solve his problems or difficulties. We are of the opinion that cumulative record cards intended for the primary classes should be very simple, so that primary teachers can use them with just a little training. In the first instance, the cards should be introduced from class IV onwards in about 10 per cent of selected schools as an experimental measure; but once the majority of teachers are trained in evaluating certain important aspects of the child's personality and the proper maintenance of the records, the use of the cards may be gradually extended to all the higher primary and, as a next step, even to lower primary schools.

### *Necessity of Primary External Examination*

At the end of the primary stage (class VII or VIII) an external examination to be taken compulsorily by all pupils was strongly recommended by some witnesses who appeared before the Commission. We were informed that some of the States which had abolished the external examination at the end of this stage had either re-introduced it or proposed re-introducing it in the near future. It was pointed out that an external examination was necessary for (1) maintaining certain uniform standards at the end of the stage; (2) providing a basis for choice of courses at the secondary stage; and (3) creating incentives for better teaching and learning. But all these arguments do not establish a case for an external examination of the formal type to be compulsorily taken by all the pupils in class VII or VIII. Though we have recommended elsewhere that the first national standard of attainment should be defined at the end of the primary stage, we do not think it necessary or desirable to prescribe a rigidly uniform level of attainment for all the primary school pupils in a State or even in a district, through an external examination. Moreover, instead of creating incentives for better teaching, the external examination intended for all will saddle teachers with standardised programmes and encourage the process of rote memorisation, which is the besetting evil of teaching and learning methods in our schools today. Again, since full-time education at the lower secondary stage will provide, by and large, general adduction without any streaming, the argument regarding the choice does not hold good; and for the diversion of pupils to full-time vocational courses to be made available at the stage, an examination which will merely test intellectual ability and academic attainment will not be of much help. Therefore, it is recommended that no compulsory external examination should be held at the completion of the primary school stage.

Though, not in favour of a compulsory external examination, we believe that for the proper maintenance of standards, periodic surveys of the level of achievement of primary schools is necessary. We recommend that such surveys should be conducted by the district educational authorities to assess the standard of performance of the schools in a given area by means of standardised or highly refined tests prepared by specialists in the State Evaluation Organisations. This procedure will enable the education officers to pick out the weaker schools and help them to improve their performance. It will also assist the schools in finding out the weakness of their pupils for purposes of reforms.

***Common Internal Examination***

With the use of the standardised or refined test material referred to above, the district educational authorities may, if they so desire, arrange for a common examination to be taken by the pupils of all the schools in a district at the end of the primary stage. This common school leaving examination will be different from the school certificate examination now held in many States, because though the question papers will be set by the district educational authorities or by special paper-setters appointed by the State Evaluation Organisation, the performance of the pupils of each participating school will be assessed by the teachers of the school themselves, and not by external examiners. The advantages of such a common final examination for the primary schools are obvious. As the question papers will contain standardised tests and highly refined and professional test items, the evaluation will be more valid and reliable than what is possible through the kind of annual and final examinations conducted in the ordinary primary school. Moreover, through such common tests inter-school comparability with regard to levels of performance in the district can be obtained, and this would be helpful, as shown above, both to the education officers and to the schools. We would like to emphasise that the question papers in the different subjects at this common examination should be or short duration, each of not more than one hour or one hour and a half, so that the entire examination should be completed in two or three days.

The main aim of the proposal is to reform the existing examination by making it less formal, reducing its burden on the pupils' minds, and increasing its validity as a measure of educational attainment. The school at the primary stage plays the determining role in the total assessment of such attainment. The certificate regarding the completion of the course should be given by the school and not by the external agency, and this certificate should be accompanied by a statement showing the results of the common final examination, if any, together with the results of the internal assessment made by the school of the pupils' performance throughout the year as shown in his cumulative records.

Besides to the common examination, special tests may be held at the end of the primary course for the award of scholarships or certificates of merit or for the purpose of identifying talent and pupils may appear for these tests on a voluntary basis. The evaluation of the examinee's performance in these tests will be done by external examiners.

### *Reforming External Examination*

At present the external examination in the case of the higher secondary class or the intermediate classes located in the school, the external examination is held by the State Board of Secondary (or Higher Secondary) Education and in the case of pre-university class, by the university concerned. We have recommended that the pre-university classes now located in affiliated colleges should be transferred to schools as higher secondary classes in a phased programme spread over ten years, and that the duration of the higher secondary course should be extended to two years everywhere by 1986. When these classes are located exclusively in the schools, the Board of School Education will conduct the external examination at the end of class XI (or class XII) as well as that at the end of class X. In the transitional period the present dual control will continue. What we state below applies to all external examinations at the school stage, whether they are at present conducted by the Boards or by the universities.

(A) The weaknesses in the present system of external examinations are due to defects in the questions and the question papers set for the examination. The paper-setters are, by and large, appointed on the basis of seniority, subject competence, and experience in teaching. Very few of them possess the necessary knowledge and skill in the construction of valid and dependable tests. We are of the opinion that no major break-through towards the improvement of external examinations is possible unless (a) the technical competence of paper-setters is raised through an intensive training programme sponsored by the State Boards; (b) the question papers are oriented to testing not merely the acquisition of knowledge but the ability to apply knowledge and the development of problem-solving abilities; and (c) the nature of the questions asked is improved.

(B) Besides the improvement of questions and question papers, many other procedures of the external examinations need to be made more systematic and scientific. For example, the marks of different subjects are added without being standardised. The determination of cut-off points, the award of grace marks and other similar methods are also not based on any sound rationale. All these factors tend to make the examinations scores less and less reliable. It is essential that scientific scoring procedures should be devised so that there may be optimum reliability in the assessment of the candidate's performance.

(c) With the ever-increasing number of students appearing for the Board examinations, the task of getting the answer scripts properly valued and of processing the results efficiently within a given time is becoming more and more difficult. It is necessary that this process should be mechanised so as to make it more accurate and expeditious.

***Failures of Large Incidence***

The matter about which the public at large is most deeply

concerned is not the irrationality of the scoring procedures or the inefficiency of the administrative processes, but the large incidence of failures in the external examination at the end of the school stage. An analysis of the results of the different Board examinations for the last five years show that about 55 per cent of the candidates appearing for the high school examination and about 40 per cent of those appearing for the, higher secondary school examination fail regularly every year. In the case of the private candidates the percentage soars up to 70 or even more. Failure often has a demoralising effect on the unsuccessful candidate. The failure of such large numbers of students, particularly after they have been screened year after year by means of annual and other school examinations, is a sad reflection on our methods of education as well as on our system of examination.

There is no doubt that if the measures suggested above for the reform of the external examination are properly implemented, the situation will gradually change in the years to come. We also believe, that with the proposed improvement in the curriculum, instructional materials and methods of teaching and the reorientation in the training of teachers, the incidence of examination failures will be reduced. But we do not think that a student should be branded as a total failure, if he passes in certain subjects but is unable to make the grade in others. There is no reason why he should carry with him the stigma of being declared an unsuccessful candidate if he has partially succeeded in his educational effort.

### *Certificates Given by the School and Board*

We recommend that the certificate issued by the Board on the basis of the results of the external examination at the end of the lower or higher secondary stage, should give the candidate's performance only in those subjects in which he has passed, but there should be no remark to the effect that he has passed or' failed in the whole examination. The Board, however, should issue a statement along with the certificate showing his marks or grades in all the subjects. We further recommend that the candidate should be permitted to appear again, if he so desires, for the entire examination or for separate subjects in order to improve his performance.

On the completion of the course, at the end of the lower or higher secondary stage, the student should receive a certificate from the school also giving the record of his internal assessment as contained in his cumulative record card. This certificate may be attached to that given by the Board in connection with the external examination. We are however of the opinion that the external examination need not be compulsory for all the students of class X or class XI/XII. A student may choose to leave the school with the school certificate only without appearing for the external examination, and seek a job or even an entry into some vocational course on the basis of the certificate and the school records. It must be recognised, however that since admission to institutions of higher secondary education as well as of higher education will be selective, the authorities controlling such institutions will lay down their own rules of eligibility for admission. A student seeing entry into these institutions may have not only to pass the external examination in the subjects laid down and secure the prescribed grades but also submit himself if necessary to certain admission tests required by the institutions.

### *Experimental Schools*

Certain measures are suggested above for reducing the domination which the external examination exercises over school education. In order to lessen its importance still further, we recommend that a few selected schools should be given the right of assessing their students themselves and holding their own final examination at the end of class X, which will be regarded at equivalent to the external examination of the State Board of School Education. The State Board will issue the certificates to the successful candidates of these schools on the recommendation of the authorise the Education Department to withdraw recognition for persistent irresponsible assessment.

### *Transitional Higher Secondary Examination*

As recommended above that the first external examination should be held at the end of class X or the first stage of schools education, and the second examination should come after class XII which will be the end of the higher secondary stage. At present, the higher secondary stage in all the State except Uttar Pradesh and Kerala ends with class XI after which there is the higher secondary school examination. This will continue to be the position till the duration of the course is extended to two years. During the transitional period, therefore, most students in the higher secondary school will have to appear for two successive external examinations, at the end of class X and class XI, within the period of a year. This is undesirable but cannot be avoided, particularly where the course of class IX, X and XI is not integrated. When the P.U.C. class gets transferred from the affiliated colleges to the high schools, the course will be a non-integrated one.

As a many existing higher secondary schools with integrated courses are already in existence in some of the States, we do not insist that this integration should be broken up and the students of the schools should be made to appear for two public examinations within a year. There may be only one public examination for such students—the higher secondary school examination at the end of class XI. However, we would like to invite attention in this connection to the procedure that is followed in some areas, where the higher secondary school examination is staggered over a period of two years, the core subjects being offered for examination at the end of class X and the electives at the end of class XI. This procedure may be adopted with suitable modifications in other places. It must be remembered that the problem 'is a temporary one and will disappear when schools are organised on the pattern of 10 plus 2.

The comprehensive evaluation programme that we have described in the preceding paragraphs requires for its implementation a well-organised machinery both at the State and the Central levels. The Secondary Boards of School Education that now conduct external examinations at the secondary stage will be converted into State Boards of School Education with enhanced powers and functions. At the Centre, there will be a National Board of School Education that will be responsible for evaluation programmes at the national level. The composition, the powers and the functions at these Boards will be considered in the next chapter.

## Summary

### *Guidance & Counselling*

Guidance and counselling should be regarded as an integral part of education, meant for all students and aimed at assisting the individual to make decisions and adjustments from time to time.

1. *Guidance at the Primary Stage.* Guidance should begin from the lowest class, in the primary school and in view of the large numbers of schools involved, the programme may be introduced through simple measures such as (a) familiarising teachers under training with diagnostic testing and the problem of individual differences; (b) organising in-service courses for primary teachers; (c) producing occupational literature ; and (d) helping pupils and parents in choice of further education.
2. *Guidance at the Secondary Stage.* Guidance at the secondary stage should, among other things, help in the identification and development of the abilities and interests of adolescent pupils. The ultimate

objective should be to introduce adequate guidance services in *all* secondary schools with a trained counsellor in charge of the programme. But in view of the limited financial and personnel resources, a short-range programme should be adopted for the next 20 years consisting of:

(a) a minimum guidance programme for all secondary schools through a visiting school counsellor for a group of ten schools, assisted by the school teachers in the simpler guidance functions;

(b) comprehensive guidance programme in selected schools, one in each district, to serve as models; and

(c) provision of necessary supervisory staff in the State Bureaux of Guidance.

3. All secondary school teachers should be introduced to guidance concepts through pre- or in-service training. The training colleges should be suitably staffed for the purpose.
4. *General.* Arrangements should be made for the professional training of guidance workers by the State Bureaux of Guidance and training colleges. Advanced training should be organised at the national level.
5. Ancillary programmes should include the production of guidance literature and materials and research into problems of guidance in the Indian situation.

### *Evaluation*

Evaluation is a continuous process, forms an integral part of the total system of education and is intimately related to educational objectives. It exercises a great influence on the pupil's study habits and the teacher's methods of instruction and thus helps not only to measure educational achievement but also to improve it.

1. *Evaluation at the Lower Primary Stage.* Evaluation at this stage should help pupils to improve their achievement in the basic skills and development of right habits and attitudes.
2. The new approach to evaluation will attempt to improve the written examination so that it becomes a valid and reliable measure of educational achievement and to devise techniques for measuring those important aspects of the student's growth that cannot be measured by written examinations.
3. It would be desirable to treat classes I to IV as an ungraded unit to enable children to advance at their own pace. Where this is not feasible, classes I and II may be treated as one block divided into two groups—one for slow and the other for fast learners. Teachers should be appropriately trained for the ungraded system.
4. *External Examination at the End of the Primary Stage.* Although the first national standard of attainment is to be set at the end of the primary stage, it is not considered necessary or desirable to prescribe a rigid and uniform level of attainment through a compulsory external examination. However, for the proper maintenance of standards, periodic surveys of the level of achievement of primary schools should be conducted by district school authorities through refined tests prepared by State Evaluation Organisations.
5. *Evaluation at the Higher Primary Stage.* In addition to written examinations, weightage should be given at this stage to oral tests as a part of internal assessment. Diagnostic testing should be through simple teacher-made tests. Cumulative record cards are important in indicating pupils' growth and development but should be very simple and should be introduced in a phased manner.

6. *A Common External Examination for Inter-School Comparability.* The district educational authority may arrange for a common examination at the end of the primary stage for schools in the district, using standardised and refined tests. This examination will have greater validity and reliability than the school examination and will provide inter-school comparability of levels of performance.
7. The certificate at the end of the primary course should be given by the school and should be accompanied by the cumulative record card and the statement of results of the common examination, if any.
8. *Higher Secondary Examination.* During the transition period, higher secondary students will have to appear for two successive external examinations—at the end of classes X and XI, within one year. Where, however, the courses in classes IX to XI are integrated, the examination at the end of class X need not be insisted upon.
9. In addition to the common examinations, special tests may be held at the end of the primary course for the award of scholarships or certificates of merit and for the purpose of identifying talent.
10. *Improvement in External Examinations.* External examinations should be improved by raising the technical competence of papersetters, orienting question papers to objectives other than to acquisition of knowledge, improving the nature of questions, adopting scientific scoring procedures, and mechanising the scoring of scripts and the processing of results.
11. *Certificate given by the Board and School.* The certificate issued by the State Board of School Education on the basis of the results of the external examination should

give the candidate's performance in different subjects for which he has appeared and there should be no remark to the effect that he has passed or failed in the whole examination. The candidate should be permitted to appear again, if he so desires, for the entire examination or for separate subjects in order to improve his performance.

12. *Establishment of Experimental Schools.* A few selected schools should be given the right of assessing their students themselves and holding their own final examination at the end of class X, which will be regarded as equivalent to the external examination of the State Board of School Education. The State Board of School Education will issue the certificates to the successful candidates of these schools on the recommendation of the schools. A committee set up by the State Board of School Education should develop carefully worked-out criteria for the selection of such schools. The schools should be permitted to frame their own curricula, prescribe their own text-books, and conduct their educational activities without external restrictions.

13. *Methods of Internal Assessment.* Internal assessment by schools should be comprehensive and evaluate all aspects of student growth including those not measured by the external examination. It should be descriptive as well as quantified. Written examinations conducted by schools should be improved and teachers trained appropriately. The internal assessment should be shown separately from the external examination marks.

### *Teaching Methods: Discovery and Diffusion*

The continual deepening of the curricula should be accomplained by an equally vigorous improvement in the method of teaching and evaluation. The main factors responsible for the dull and uninspiring school teaching today are the rigidity of the educational system and the failure of the administrative machinery to diffuse new educational practices to schools. These weeknesses should be overcome.

1. *Elasticity and Dynamism.* A good educational system should be dynamic, flexible and discriminating enough to help institutions and teachers to proceed along different levels of development—the good schools be free to go ahead on creative and experimental lines while the weaker ones should be supported to gain a sense of security.
2. Such elasticity and dynamism are possible if the experimenting teacher is supported by the administrative authority, a general atmosphere of reform, the encouragement of the head of the institution, a mastery of subject-matter, leadership provided by training institutions, and the availability of teaching materials.
3. Elasticity in a school system will have little value if new practices developed are not diffused to schools and: schools. A committee set up by the State Board of School Education should develop carefully worked-out criteria for the selection of such schools. The schools should not only be freed from the requirements of an external examination but should be permitted to frame their own curricula, prescribe their own textbooks, and conduct their educational activities without departmental restrictions.

This is a bold step in the direction of freedom and of educational experimentation. But the right given to the experimental schools should be reviewed periodically as institutions invested with such powers should continuously earn their privilege. We hope, however, that after the experiment is tried out successfully in a few schools, more and more schools will be released from the restrictive influence of the external examination and given the freedom to work out their own ideas in education.

*Methods of Internal Assessment:* We shall now pass on to the question of internal assessment to which a reference was made earlier in this section. This internal assessment or evaluation conducted by individual schools is of great significance and should be given increasing importance. It should be comprehensive, evaluating all those aspects of the student's growth that are measured by the external examination and also those personality traits, interests and attitudes which cannot be assessed by it. Internal assessment should be built into the total educational programme of the school and should be used for improvement rather than for certifying the level of achievement of the student. It must be pointed out that all items of internal assessment need not follow qualified scoring procedures. Some of them may be assessed in descriptive terms. The results should be kept separately and not be combined artificially with other results to form aggregate scores.

The written examinations conducted in schools should be improved on the same lines as the external examination. The use of standardised achievement tests, wherever available, is strongly recommended. There is need for developing other types of evaluation tools for improving internal assessment such as interest inventories, aptitude tests and rating scales. They should be prepared by specialists and made available to schools, and the teachers should be trained to use them through a network of in-service programmes. Teachers should also be trained to make simple tests of their own on the models supplied and use them for the assessment of the performance of their pupils.

We are aware that the experience of introducing internal assessment has not been very happy so far and that there has been persistent over-assessment by the weaker schools. This has led some critics to suggest that the system should be abandoned altogether. We cannot agree with this view. Internal assessment has to continue and its importance will have to be increasingly emphasised. To overcome the shortcomings discovered, we make the following recommendations:

1. The results of the internal assessment and external' examination should not be combined because the purposes and techniques of the two evaluations are different and because the results of the internal assessment of the different institutions are not strictly comparable. The results of the external and internal assessment should, therefore, be shown separately in the certificate(s) given at the end of the course.
2. It should be an important point in the inspections of schools to review the internal assessment made and to examine the correlation between the internal and external assessments. Persistence in over-assessment should be regarded as a weakness in the school programmes. It should be taken due note of while classifying the schools and should also be related to grants-in-aid so that institutions which tend to over-assess their students persistently would stand to lose in status and finance. The grant-in-aid rules should also teachers given skilled help in trying out innovations. The educational administration can encourage and hasten the diffusion of new teaching methods by: combining permissiveness with persuasion; approaching the new methods in stages according to the ability of schools; giving necessary in-service training to teachers; and, providing adequate guide materials which should be constantly revised and improved.

At the same time the administrator has to guard himself against letting any 'progressive' measure settling down into another orthodoxy.

***Class Size***

1. Classes of somewhat larger size than what is strictly considered as desirable cannot be avoided in our country for a long time. However, it is necessary to restrict the number of pupils admitted to each class to a maximum of 50 in the lower primary, 45 in the higher primary and lower secondary, and 40 in higher secondary classes.
2. *Multiple-class Teaching*. Training institutions should orient teachers to these techniques. Research be undertaken in the problems and techniques of multiple-class teaching.

***Issues of Textbooks, Teachers' Aids***

1. One of the key programme is provision of quality textbooks and other teaching-learning materials for raising standards at comparatively low cost.
2. At the national level a comprehensive programme of textbook production should be implemented by mobilising the best talent in the country on the lines already being attempted by NCERT in India. Such books will facilitate the definition and practical indication of expected standards. National integration will be enhanced by this.
3. The effort at the national level should be supported and augmented by each State setting up an expert section for the production of textbooks.
4. The Ministry of Education should take steps to establish in the public sector an autonomous organisation, functioning on commercial lines for the production of textbooks at the national level, especially scientific

and technical books. A small committee may be set up to work out the details of the project.

5. The preparation, try-out and evaluation of textbooks should be the responsibility of the State Education Departments. The production aspect of the textbooks may preferably be done by the State Education Departments, wherever possible, through their own textbook presses. The sale and distribution of textbooks are better left to the student cooperatives and not be assumed directly by the Departments.
6. Textbooks and teaching aids production at the State level should preferably be entrusted to an autonomous agency functioning in close liaison with the Education Department.
7. Arrangements should be made that the textbooks are subjected to continuous revision and improvement.
8. At least 2 or 3 books should be provided in each subject to provide a multiple choice of books for the schools.
9. Policies adopted should be liberal for remunerating authors suitably.
10. The entire organisation of State production of text-books should be run on a no-profit-no-loss basis.
11. Manuscripts should be invited from a variety of sources including teachers, and a high-level committee of professional persons should select and approve manuscripts.
12. Teachers' guides and other instructional material should supplement textbooks.
13. Minimum required teaching aids and equipment needed by each category of schools should be listed and steps taken to provide the equipment to every school, on a high priority basis.

14. Broadcasting of special radio talks specially designed for teachers in the mornings and evenings will help teachers in lesson preparation. Sophisticated forms of newer techniques would not be suitable at present in the general run of schools but may be tried out experimentally in teacher-training institutions. Education Departments should work with the All-India Radio for the use of radio lessons, supplemented by printed guide materials for teachers and pupils.
15. Teachers should be helped and trained to rely on inexpensive and locally available or improvised teaching aids. Costly equipment available neighbourhood should be shared by schools.

### *Towards School Buildings*

1. In view of the present gloomy position regarding school buildings, it is necessary retake steps to clear the backlog of unconstructed school buildings as well as to provide additional buildings for new enrolment.
2. Allocations for construction of school buildings should be increased in the Central and State budgets, and community resources mobilised on the basis of equalisation. Loans and grants-in-aid should be given on a liberal basis to private schools for the construction of buildings.
3. *Cost Reduction.* The norms and guidance already available for spacing and planning of school buildings should be put into practice.
4. In view of the shortage of traditional building material and the cost involved, well-designed and constructed *kacha* structures should be accepted as part of the school system.
5. *School Buildings in Rural Areas.* In rural areas, efforts should be made to encourage local initiative and contribution in putting up school buildings. The

'nucleus' approach suggested by the Ministry of Education is recommended for general adoption.

6. *Buildings in Urban Areas.* Economy in these buildings should be effected by using locally available materials, omission of certain finishes, and acceptance of a lower standard of construction. Temporary structures may be used, wherever possible, and improved techniques of construction may be adopted in putting up pucka buildings.
7. *Expeditious Construction.* In order to accelerate provision of school buildings, construction in rural areas may be entrusted to local communities or village panchayats, and in urban areas, municipalities and corporations may be utilised for the purpose.
8. For supervision and to guide the programme of construction of school buildings and introduce improved techniques, an Educational Building Development Group should be set up in each State within the Public Works Department and working in close association with the Education Department. These groups will standardise details of construction in the region so as to make possible the mass production of the components on a factory scale. A similar Building Development Group should be set up at the Centre for coordination.
9. The economy measures worked out by the Educational Building Development Group should be made known to private institutions and grants-in-aid given on the upper cost limits basis.

***Search and Development***

1. The search for talent must be a continuous process, pursued at all stages, but the secondary stage is the most crucial.
2. Besides the programmes of enrichment and advanced

curricula, a variety of extra-mural programmes should be organised for the talented such as summer schools, visits to places of educational interest and provision of hostels and day centres for those whose home environment is not conducive to study.

3. For providing an atmosphere for free expression and creative work, teachers should be oriented to the special techniques of dealing with the talented children.

# Appendices

## APPENDIX - I

### THE COURSE OF EDUCATIONAL TECHNOLOGY

[In India, Educational Technology is also being given a serious consideration. Here we are reproducing the proceeding of an effort at Govt.'s Level. We owe deep sense of gratitude to Course Coordinator for this.—Ed].

The course was intended for teacher educators working in the field of Educational Technology in universities, training colleges as well as key level persons in audio-visual departments of States SCERT. There were about 20 seats for this course. Out of 41 applicants, 20 participants were selected for this course. Finally 14 participants from various states—Gujarat, Madhya Pradesh, Maharashtra, Rajasthan, Jammu and Kashmir, Uttar Pradesh and Union Territory of Delhi participated (list enclosed in appendix).

The main purpose of the course was to orient participants towards educational technology and its various dimensions (theoretical and practical) so that they in turn could train teachers in their "respective institutions. To meet this purpose, a lot of preparatory work was done for formulating the course-objectives and course-contents. Firstly draft course content along with objectives was prepared. This was finalised in five successive meetings with all Heads of Divisions of CIET under the Chairmanship of Joint-Director, Besides this, time plan for each lecture/demonstration/practicum was also planned. In order to provide background of the course to participants in advance, briefs of each lecture practicum was also prepared in consultation with resource persons from faculty of C.I.E.T. Training booklet consisting of course content, objectives, Time plan, briefs of lectures and resource persons along with reading list of important books was also prepared.

**Objectives**

The specific objectives of the course were as follows: To familiarise participants with the

(i) theoretical framework viz. concept, sub-system and scope of educational technology (ET).
(ii) characteristics and potential of different types of Graphics aids and media (small format and Mass)
(iii) process of development of different types of Graphics aids, Audio/Radio and ETV programmes.
(iv) hardware (equipment) used in the production of tape slide/Radio-audio, ETV programmes.
(v) practical experiences in preparation of instructional materials/scripts used for different types of Graphic-aids/media.
(vi) the utilisation, evaluation and dissemination of various types of broadcasting & non-broadcasting programmes.

**Course Content**

On the basis of above mentioned objectives, the modular form of course content was formulated. The course was devided into five modules and project work.

*Module I* — Theoretical Framework of Educational Technology
*Module II* — Graphics.
*Module III* — Audio/Radio Programmes
*Module IV* — ETV Programmes

*Module V* — Information & Dissemination

*Module VI* — Project work for production of tapeslides, audio/video programmes using principles of educational Technology.

**Design**

The course was designed in such a way so that balance between theoretical and practical dimension of Educational Technology could be maintained. The first half of the course was devoted towards theoretical aspects of E.T. which included lecture demonstration and preview of tapeslide, Radio/audio and ETV programmes. Educational tour was also arranged. The second half of the course was utilised for practical work which consisted of script writing and production of tapeslide, audio and video programmes. Audio programme could not be produced due to some other courses in educational Radio Division of the institute during that period. The last day was planned for evaluation of the course and summing up session.

## PROCEEDINGS OF THE COURSE

### *Summary Reports of Day to Day Activities*

**31st January 1989**

The course commenced with a welcome and introduction of the participants as well as the resource persons.

Dr. M.C. Sharma Coordinator of the Course... highlighted the objectives of the course. He stressed that the course is intended to orient the teacher educators towards the theoretical dimensions of educational technology. Accordingly the participants would be exposed to the hardware as well as preparation of software & programme production in educational technology.

Prof. J.S. Rajput, Head, Eductional Script Training & SIET

Coordination, CIET, in his keynote address spoke about the need of educational technology in our educational system in the context of New Education policy. He said that the actual success of this course would depend on the follow-up activities to be taken up by the participants in their respective areas/ institutions.

Prof. C.H.K. Misra... further clarified the concept of educational technology and how it stands today. According to him the concept needs a lot of clarity as well as optimistic approach. There was sharing of expectations among the resource persons and the participants. The participants individually gave some ideals about their experience in educational technology and what they expected from this course. The faculty members also desired a "total involvement" of the participants.

## MODULE I

Prof. Mishra initiated certain basic questions about the teaching learning process like why (purpose) and what (content) to teach, how (method) to teach which incorporates—the method, media and techniques. The difference between the method and media marked out. The importance of sequencing and its relevance to the target audience was pointed out. From the broad purpose of instruction, the specific objectives are drawn. Based on these lines, educational technology is a structured and planned way of instruction. Still it is a flexible approach to incorporate self-evaluation and correction. Thus, it is a dynamic approach demanding a purposeful a utilisation of all resources available in a particular instructional situation.

Dr. Mullick introduced the 'Systems Approach' as a method of analysing, planning and evaluating a process as well as a problem solving approach. A system is viewed as an enterprise consisting of men and material to achieve certain purpose. A system is characterised by the parameters like (i) input (ii) process and (iii) output in its environmental functionalities and constraints. The objective of the systems approach is optimisation of all the components which are linked with each other. Systems approach helps to have a wholistic, rational way of solving problems by analysing the components or subsystems and their relations with each other. The examples of formal and nonformal system of education were given to signify the difference between the functionalities although the components are same.

Shri Chandra Bhushan conducted the first session after lunch on communication. The participants inductively arrived at the definition of the term. The process of communication was built up on the basis of questions like who says what, on what channel, to whom and with what results? Delineating the various activities carried out by the teacher, the communication is ideal when the gulf between the teacher and the learner is minimised.

The participants were shown a short film produced by CIET. "Castles in the air". It was followed by the views of the participants regarding the message it conveyed, whether the situations to convey the message were appropriate and the target audience. According to the views expressed by the participants the film intended to create an awareness to the depleting natural resources and gradual deterioration of the environment.

**1st February, 1989**

The day commenced at 10 a.m. with a short summary of the previous day's proceedings.

Dr. Misra in his summing up emphasised on two major points—

1. Communication is a people process.

2. Intended message and the real message have a gap and ET aims to bridge this gap.

He later on outlined the Instructional Technology system (ITS). In this system the focal points were.

1. Insistance on optimisation of the different components of the system.
2. Planning is done backwards while instruction proceeds forward.
3. Optimisation could be done only by empirical testing. No fixed formula or guidelines could be drawn on how to optimise.

In the next session Dr. M.C. Sharma dealt at length on Instructional Models and their applications in Instruction. At the outset he underlined the necessity for an Instructional Model—that is was a set of plans which could provide guidelines for designing instruction to achieve certain goals.

The different Instructional models were:

1. Social Interaction Model.
2. Personal Model.
3. Modification Interaction Model.
4. Information Processing Model.

From the point of view of ET, Information Processing was the most important. Under this category, there are three models—

(a) Burner's concept Attainment Model.
(b) Asubel's Advance Organiser Model.
(c) Taba's Enquiry Model.

Dr. Sharma outlined the various features of Bruner's and Asubel's Models. While Bruners emphasised thinking *Strategies* in the attainment of concept. In view of Asubel it was *meaningful learning* which was important, the best strategy according to Bruner was conservative focussing. The syntax of three of his models.

1. Reception model.
2. Selection Model.
3. Unarranged Material.

Was presented. The syntax of Asubel's Advance Organiser Model was also shown. Both Bruner's and Asubel's Models were illustrated with examples. The Enquiry model was incorporated in both Bruner's and Asubel's models.

In third pre-lunch session, Dr. Mullick conducted a practicum session on the application of systems approach for solving Educational Problems.

The specific problem chosen was improving the performance of students of a rural school and with reference to this, the systems approach was applied to find out the Educational problems. Problems were envisaged by the participants in the areas of human resources, materials and learners. A number of problems in the three areas were put forth. Some of them were

1. Motivation of teachers.
2. Poor Coordination between the teachers, Headmasters and the other backup agencies.
3. Multiple-class teaching.
4. Back of teacher-parent interaction.
5. Less of community involvement.
6. Lack of optimisation of the use of existing materials available.
7. Difficulty in the access to available material.

Dr. Mullick also dealt with other specific examples to clarify some aspects. At the end of the session, all the participants were given an assignment where the problem was to optimise the use of Audio-Visual Resources available in our institutes.

The first post-lunch session was devoted to a discussion on-Research areas in ET. Dr. J. Singh highlighted some of the research areas. For this, he first divided the field of ET into-two areas.

1. Technology in Education
   — dealing with hardware
2. Technology of Education
   — software—process and development systems approach.

In *the field of hardware* the following were possible research areas.

1. A survey or census of agencies producing hardware suppliers of hardware and availability of hardware.
2. Present status with respect to
   — availability of materials.
   — supply agencies.
   — availability of training courses/agencies
3. Future projection
   — This area dealt with prediction of the hardware requirements for the future.
4. Cost effective studies/Economics of different hardwares.

In the *field of process and development of software* the possible research areas are:

1. Feed forward research. This included research in

— diagnostic findings of needs by participant-observation.
— audience profile.

2. Formative research
— testing of the script before formalisation.

3. Testing
— in ETV programmes.
— Content analysts

In the *field of systems analysis* possible research areas-were:

1. In summative evaluation of materials.
2. Evaluation of the system itself.

This could be done by case study method or Experimental method.

The final session of the day was a practicum on the Evaluation of an ETV programme conducted by Dr. Kanade.

The participants were shown a "15 minute film" which was made by the C.I.E.T. as a part of the mass Orientation programme for the teachers.

After the film was shown the participants were given an exercise on evaluating the film. They were asked to comment on:

1. Aim/message of the film.
2. Comment on 12 aspects of the film.
3. Comment on the same 12 aspects using a rating scale.
4. Using the same proforma in groups.

Dr. Kanade explained the difficulties faced by the investigator in analysing such a large number of response and also showed by way of examples how the data could be collected and analysed in a simple and systematic manner and audience-profiles made.

**2nd February, 1989**

The previous day's report was presented. After that Dr. C.H.K. Misra while talking on the production of Video films said that three main purpose of the film must be kept in mind:

1. The film should properly convey the message.
2. It should relate past experiences of the audience with the present and the future.
3. It should entertain.

## MODULE II

Dr. T.R. Bawa took the first part of his lecture on Graphics in Education. After briefly outlining the history of E.T. and its future prospects, he explained the importance of using Graphics particularly in a developing country like India With limited resources. The advantages of Graphic aids explained were:

— Their attractiveness
— Their inexpensiveness
— Ease of preparation
— Ease of use
— Portability

Guidelines on how to plan and prepare Graphic Instructional material were also given. Some of them were:

1. Clarity of message.
2. Try out of several approaches to presentation.
3. Pictorial Thinking.
4. Use of colour.

A number of examples were shown on how these principles could be applied.

A session on "Blackboard" was conducted by Dr. S.P. Mullick. The participants were given a book entitled "Operation blackboards—a project" and the types of black-boards illustrated in the book were discussed with reference to their advantages and disadvantages. Some suggestions on new types of blackboards which could be made, were made by some participants. Mr. K.K. Chainani was also present during this session and made some valuable suggestions.

A session on "Visual communication" was conducted by Shri K.K. Chainani. He outlined the salient features of visual communication and emphasised that a combination of different strokes make visual. Every feature was illustrated by a number of examples. All the features illustrated were again combined and shown on a visual entitled "A boy going to school". This was worked out on the black board and different combinations of strokes, mater in the visual and those were suggested by the participants in making an effective visual.

In the last session of the day Dr. Harmesh Lal discussed the "Low cost teaching aids". Giving a brief outline of the project taken up in 1977 by the Deptt. of teaching aids (NCERT) in Madhya Pradesh, he stressed on the need for use of these teaching aids especially in rural primary schools. Two-films "Low cost teaching aids" were shown. While evaluating the films, some basic questions were raised:

1. Are low-cost teaching aids really low cost?
2. Do some low cost aids distract the concept like the example of making geometrical figures?

Based on this, a discussion led to the question on whether the philosophy behind the production of low cost teaching aids was right. Dr. M.C. Sharma then explained the basic philosophy behind low cost teaching aids.

**3rd February 1989**

After the presentation of the previous a day's report, Dr. Misra spoke briefly on the concept of Simulogy. Then Dr. Bawa, conducted on the second part of the lecture on Graphic Aids where he elaborated on the use of charts. The following aspects were discussed.

1. Purpose of Charts.
2. Characteristics of Charts.
3. Types of Charts.
   — Flowchart.
   — Tree Chart.
   — Data Chart.
   — Flip Chart.
   — Strip Chart.

Each type of chart was discussed and illustrated with examples:

A session on "Tape-slide material in Education" was taken up by Shri K.K. Chainani. The blue-print of making a slide was discussed with all technical details. This was followed by the viewing of a films trip on "How to make a hand-made film-strip" and on "Silk screen printing".

In the afternoon, various tape slide programmes were screened for the participants which were then evaluated. The tape slide programmes were:

1. 3 tape slide programmes of a five part series on Population Education.
2. Covalent and Ionic bond.

While evaluating the Population Education Programme, some of the views expressed were:

1. Visual were powerful with excellent photography.

2. The message was accurately conveyed.
3. Use of colours in showing different statistics was effective.

After the tape-slide programme on covalent and Tonic bond was viewed. The following observations were made:

1. Too many concepts were covered.
2. An understanding for the colours used in the visuals to denote difficult symbols was not shown.

To the observation that too many concepts were covered, Dr. M.C. Sharma pointed out that this programme of 40 slides could be broken up into smaller units and then covered in 3 or 4 parts.

**6th February, 1989**

After the presentation of report, Dr. Misra clarified some aspects of simulogy at a request from the participants. He defined simulogy as a science of signification. Simulogy's features were:

— Signs without language could communicate.
— "Places" signified different things.
— Men and material could be manipulated to signify something.

## MODULE III

**ETV in India**

Dr. M.M. Chaudhri traced the History of ETV transmission in India. Referring to its development in the past 30 years. Since Delhi started the first school broadcast in 1959, Dr. Chaudhri said that ETV transmission had come a long way. At present the UGC programmes were 50% imported and 50% indigeneous but the ETV programmes for schools produced by CIET were 100% indigeneous. ETV in India could be divided into 4 different units:

1. Training
2. Production Facilities.
3. Transmission
4. Access.

The major problems at present were in the field of training and in making ETV accessible to the viewers.

ETV had a major role to play in being able to provoke thinking, in making the viewers creative and in making them solve problems. A healthy coordination was necessary between, the medium, content and audience.

### *ETV Curriculum—Need and Preparation*

Dr. Misra in the session on ETV curriculum said that the Educational Philosophy on which the curriculum was based was most important. According to him curriculum is based largely on four philosophies.

1. Perennialism
   — Education is to convey the basic truths.
2. Essentialism
   — to bring out the prominent "essential" elements and all educational details to be put in terms of those elements.
3. Purposivism
   — emphasis on meaningfulness in real life.
4. Constructivism.
   — Education should teach the student to construct again, to challenge every basic truth, create problems, and solve them.

These philosophies were further elaborated in terms of

the general goals, specific goals and objectives. He felt that an ETV programme has to teach students how to think reason and how to approach life and the ETV curriculum has to be thought of well in advance.

At the end of the session, the participants were divided into two groups and a subject "Dangers of Smoking" was given to each group. A curriculum outline for a 5 minute TV film was to be prepared by each group. The target audience for one group was students between 9 and 14 years and for the other group the audience was a group of teachers.

**Communication by TV**

Shri Chandra Bhushan while talking on Educational communication by TV, traced the history of TV communication in the world and in India. He then informed the participants on how communication satellites were developed. The strengths and weaknesses of TV were discussed at length. He again emphasised the selection of the best media would depend on the content/subject. This was, stressed on and then demonstrated with the help of an exercise. The participants were given a questionnaire "Media Selection Quiz". In that a list of subjects was given and the participants were asked to select the best media for that particular subject. The responses of all the participants were then analysed to arrive at the best media needed for that subject.

**7th February, 1989**

After the presentation of report, Dr. Jagdish Singh gave the detailed transmission network of Indian Television through INSAT-IB. While emphasising the need for more transmission time for ETV programmes, he informed the participants that with INSAT-IC having come into force as a stand by to INSAT-IB and with a series of INSAT-II satellites in the near future, ETV transmission would be given a complete separate channel.

The first formal session of the day was Shri G.D. Shukul's session on "Script Writing for ETV". In Developing a script from an idea the following problems could be faced:

1. Difficulty in translating the idea into a script.
2. Workability of ideas.
3. Production effort—while writing a script, the following points should be kept in mind:
   (a) The script should be within the framework of the set objective.
   (b) It must be capable of attracting audience attention.
   (c) It must inspire production.
   (d) The best format for script should be chosen.
   (e) Shri Shukul then outlined the various steps in script writing viz.:
      (a) Selection of Theme.
      (b) Outline of Script.
      (c) Final Script.

In his conclusion, he felt that a script writer for ETV must be acquainted with the production processes so as to know the technical limitations of T.V.

**Techniques and Formats—Script Writing**

Dr. S.P. Banyal explained the various techniques and formats used in ETV script writing. The different formats which could be used were:

1. Drama.
   — Play
   — Story telling
   — Musicals
   — Dance
   — Serial
   — Series.

2. Documentary.
   — Commuted
   — Sponsored
   — On nature; geography.
3. Interview.
4. Quiz.
5. Newscast.
6. Magazine.
7. Commercials/advertisements.

Dr. Banyal elaborated on the various formats and explained that the choice of a format depended on the content. The salient features of the formats were explained with the help of two films which were screened.

The post lunch session on script writing was conducted by three resources persons—Shri G.D. Shukul, Ms. Madhu Pant and Dr. Manjula Mathur. The participants were divided into four groups and each group was asked to select a topic for script-writing and present an outline with reference to the following:

1. Target Audience.
2. Duration.
3. Broad Objectives.
4. Specific Objectives.
5. Content.
6. Format to be used.

The topics chosen by the four groups were:

1. Water Pollution—Its causes and effects.
2. Health-Education for You.
3. Operation of Set Theory.
4. What is Educational Technology.

**9th February, 1989**

Dr. Jagdish Singh and Dr. M.C. Sharma answered some querries on script-writing after the presentation of the report. Some of the points highlighted were:

— Audience interaction is essential before producing a script.
— There should be no factual errors.
— Ideas should be repeated in the script at regular intervals for reinforcement.
— Drastic jumps from one idea to another should not be incorporated in a script. At every stage, a relaxation period should be given.

### *Educational Communication by TV*

The entire process of an ETV production was explained in detail by Shri Chandra Bhushan. Laying emphasis on the fact that TV production was a people's process, he said that the good coordination between the physical infrastructure and the people would lead to a good production. The elements of a TV Production were elaborated as:

1. Ideas.
2. Resources which included:

**Visual**

(a) Pictures/graphics/captions.
(b) Things.
(c) People.
(d) Film Excerpts.
(e) Places.
(f) Set and light.

**Audio**

Sound/Music

3. The Language of TV (Visual Language).

   This included

   — Different Camera shots.

   — Devices/transitions.

The different Camera shots were illustrated by Mr. Gupta, Cameraman with a camera and using the participants as subjects so that they would watch it on the monitor.

### *Hardware in TV*

The second session of the morning was devoted to discussing the various hardware (equipments used in T.V.) by Mr. A.S. Tyagi. He explained that the main problem with too sophisticated equipments was that they became reduntant or outdated very soon, for example the format of a VTR changed every 4 years and that of a camera every 6 years. Due to this serting up a studio in an educational institution would be a problem because the heavy investment in hardware would become useless if the equipment becomes outdated.

He explained the various VIR's and cameras used in TV production today and explained the advantages and disadvantages of each. He also gave the price range of different equipments available in the Indian market and worked out the cost of setting up a small studio. Mr. Tyagi also gave some guidelines on purchasing VTR's and cameras.

The post-lunch session was again devoted to discuss the elements of ETV production. Mr. Chandra Bhushan elaborated, on other aspects of TV language like the floor manager's signals. The floor manager, Mr. Sharma illustrated the use of various signals used in a studio during production. The process of converting the draft script into a camera script was explained using many examples by Mr. Chandra Bhushan. Other aspects of production like the use of camera cards, blocking of shots, recce, the producer's role in arranging for resources like—visual resources, talent, technical and financial resources were also discussed.

The above aspects were than highlighted with the help of three films shown to the participants. The films shown were "special effects in film", "Words and Pictures" and "the making of a live TV film".

**9th February, 1989**

***Evaluation of ETV Programmes***

Dr. Jagdish Singh discussed at length on evaluation of ETV programmes. Heat the outset, differentiated between research and Evaluation. The following points were put forth:

1. Purpose of evaluation is to improve and not to prove.
2. All evaluation should be objective based.
3. Evaluation is suggestive.
4. Evaluative methods depend on the type of audience.

Dr. Kanade later explained the practical aspects of ETV evaluation. He pointed out a difference between traditional evaluation and evaluation in E.T. In traditional evaluation the teacher was evaluated whereas in E.T., the audience evaluates the teachers and methods. He further illustrated how difficult it was to evaluate any qualitative aspect while it was relatively easy to evaluate any aspect which was concrete. He then conducted an exercise to illustrate this point by asking the participants to judge the distance between two cities and then define the concept of violence. From the responses of the participants he demonstrated that though the distance between two cities could be judged with a certain degree of accuracy, a qualitative concept like "Violence" could not be defined very accurately as a certain element of subjectivity crept in.

The participants were given the opportunity to attend a demonstration of "Computer Graphics" by a team of experts from France. The experts said that Graphics could be used to great effect in education for Mathematics, Natural Science and Geography. Different animation techniques were shown like separation, manipulation, picture-by-picture animation, interpolation were shown some computer graphics of 3D animation were also viewed. The experts discussed with the large audience about the training period needed to master the technique and other details like cost per programme etc.

In the post-lunch session, Dr. Harmesh Lal talked on the various features of ETV transmission. He described the role of C.I.E.T. and S.I.E.T. is in the production, transmission and evaluation of ETV programmes. The programmes were sent in a capsule and a capsule consisted of the tape of programme of 45 minutes, a cue-sheet and a transmission schedule which was sent in advance to the teachers. Later on capsule prepared by C.I.E.T. was shown to the participants.

The process of editing an ETV film was explained to the participants in the editing room by Sh. Taneja and Mrs. Pushpalata. The basic requirements in editing like two monitors a master tape, process of deleting portions, transferring of audio-video from one tape to the master tape was also demonstrated.

The theoretical aspects of editing were then discussed with Sh. Chandra Bhushan. He explained the process of editing which essentially meant joining the different shots in a meaningful sequence. This required extreme patience and was a time consuming process. Editing was done as per the requirement of the producer's script. Editing could be done by the producer himself or by a professional editor.

**10th February, 1989**

Mr. Chandra Bhushan clarified some aspects of the techniques of animation in a question-answer session. He pointed out that the characters and situations in animation are unreal. He differentiated between the various types of animation like paper animation, cut out animation and film animation.

## MODULE IV

**Information and Dissemination**

Prof. Verma in his lecture on "Information and Dissemination" at the outset, emphasised the need for information. He gave statistics of how print material like periodicals, newspapers and documents had more than doubled in ten years. He then listed the various sources of Information and how information could be stored. With regard to dissemination, Prof. Verma felt that a major hurdle was that there was no cultural change in the thinking of the present librarians and this was essential as there was to be a radical change in the process of dissemination. He then elaborated on the various methods of disseminating information and showed various types of documents that could be prepared in disseminating Information.

The function, purpose and availability of material at the media resource centre was also discussed by Prof. Verma.

Dr. Kanade also concluded his lecture on evaluation and also gave examples of advanced Information technology in other countries.

The participants visited the Central Production Centre (CPC) and Media Communication Research Centre. Two senior personnel of the Centre, Mr. Thygarajan and Mr. Nag took the participants around. The CPC has two studios A and B with all the latest equipments available in the world in the field of T.V. production. Four sophisticated Cameras and light upto 500 kw (which can be electronically monitored, through a console) are there for every studio. Each studio has a production control room (PCR) where all special effects can be monitored, an audio room (with 24 channels), a paint box (for computerised graphics) and an advanced digital library system (DLS). The post production facilities available at the CPC were also shown to the participants. The CPC is used only for special programmes and it is not open to use for outsiders.

**13th February, 1989**

After the report presentation, Dr. C.H.K. Misra talked about the role of an educational technologist. He said that for a social change to occur a critical massage is necessary. The continuum of technology extends from minimal technology to ideal technology and there is a parallel continuum of minimal target to ideal target.

The scripts on "Dangers of Smoking" were then discussed and some revisions were suggested by Dr. Misra.

Dr. Rajput discussed the curriculum of ETV programme. He talked about the levels of curriculum viz. ideal, formal perceived, operational and experimental levels. Two approaches to curriculum development were discussed i.e. through environment and through relationships. Through the environmental approach, the real life situation could be investigated and in the relationship approaches—change, knowledge, values and aesthetics were the four dynamic elements.

Two video films—one on Friction and the other on Bernoulli's principles were screened and the formats of the two scripts were discussed.

In the afternoon, the participants were divided into four groups. Three groups opted to work on scripts for ETV programmes and the fourth group, decided to work on a script for a tape slide programme. The groups then worked, on formulating a content outline for the scripts on the basis of the subject/topic chosen by them.

**14th February, 1989**

After the previous day's report was read, Prof. Misra stressed the importance of educational technology as a process of instructional strategy. He emphasised that in our country education should have better access and better application through media. It should not be costly. To make educational technology serve our country (i) It should be a team work (ii) It should emphasise software over hardware and (iii) while choosing a topic, the main criteria should be that it should reach the poorest of poor students.

He also stressed that, since manpower is precious in educational technology, certain qualities have to be there in an educational technologist. An educational technologist should be a detailed minded person and he should be non-egoistic. He should have a scientific temper and he must be a participative and active member of the team. In an educational persuit, everything should be open to questions. He also said that parallel to instructional strategy is the social change. One has to act for a social change and not wait for it to happen. Only a critical mass of workers who are aware of this, can change the situation.

Dr. M.C. Sharma introduced Dr. L.G. Sumitra, Mrs. Swarna Gupta and Dr. Sarojini Pritam, a 3-member team of the Educational Radio Division. The session started in the form of team teaching.

Dr. Sumitra explained that broadcast of Radio/audio programmes for schools have been on the air for over forty years, but studies have shown that there is non-utilisation of these programmes or there is a gap in using this media. This was attributed to limited transmission time, non-suitability of listening time, non-linking of programme with the particular topics attitude of the teacher towards the programme as superfluous and ignoring the programmes. Besides, it has to be a highly localised medium. The main blame for this has been on the educationists.

In order to overcome these difficulties, it was suggested that there should be a proper coordination among the AIR,. CIET, SIET and ET Cells, it should be need based and there should be a uniform time-table to fit in the programmes.

The post-coffee session was conducted by Mr. S Gupta on process of production and techniques of radio programmes. The question raised ... was "How can we make this media reach?" Here she emphasised that the process of Radio Audio production should involve—

Firstly the *planning stage* where objectives of a concerned idea have to be formulated. The need assessment is also an important fact which includes audience research and curriculum awareness.

(2) *The development stages* consists of identification of areas development of brief. In this stage, attention span & other factors have to be kept in mind to make the programme successful. During development of a brief-objectives, target groups, subject areas etc. have to be kept in mind.

(3) The *scripting stag* The brief was discussed thoroughly with the writer before writing the script. Mrs. Gupta emphasised that during scripting stage-language, sequence, presentation, clarity of ideas, music effects and several other aspects are to

be remembered because the greatest advantage of sound lies in its direct appeal to the imagination.

(4) *The evaluation stage:* Finally the script has to be evaluated to see if it fulfils all the objectives. An audio programme on "Sangeet" made with Ustad A.A. Khan, which was produced to introduce the concept of ragas to 5+ age group was played. It was an unscripted programme and for this, selection of a spontaneous person who can create an impact on the audience was important.

The afternoon session was on scripting and formats of radio/audio programmes by Dr. Sarojini Pritam. She discussed the different types of formats used in writing a radio script. She said that to make an educational programme through broadcast a success, it should be done through proper devices. A format becomes necessary because of the need. It should be communicated properly in an interesting manner. And should not be a burden on the mind of the children.

Several audio programmes having different formats were played to enhance that

1. Audio scripts should be authentic, full of information and interesting;
2. Should not contain too many points;
3. Should encourage children to be mentally involved in the programmes; and
4. Various techniques of script writing should be used effectively to repeat ideas in the programmes.

Audio programmes were played on nursery rhymes, Ekalavya' and on the concept of measurement (without music) and those which were produced by teachers and trainees.

**15th February, 1989**

The morning session started at 9.30 a.m. in the Mother

School Wing. It was addressed by Prof. Mrs. Shukla who talked on "Evaluation of Audio Broadcasts". She stressed on the need for designing an audio programme skillfully and best suited for the learners. She pointed out that while the print media had the facility of a priority evaluation, the electronic media suffered from the limitation imposed on it by the media itself and therefore evaluation became an important factor. She suggested that the production activity should be detailed and no loose ends left before going, into actual production. Language, modality of presentation, delivery and tape quality should be very closely monitored. Audio tapes were then played for the participants. The participants were asked to evaluate the programmes and different view points were put forth in the group discussion.

In afternoon session the participants were taken around the audio studio and the different hardware used were shown to them by Mr. Bhushan. Dr. Sumitra then gave detailed guidelines on how the script for an audio programme should written. The participants were then asked to write a script for pupil teachers on "How to use audio programmes in the classroom". After the draft scripts were written,... they were analysed and discussed. Dr. Sumitra felt that in audio programmes simple words should be used so that communication would not be difficult.

**16th February, 1989**

After presentation of the reports of previous day activities by participant Dr. Misra asked each group to present two objectives of their programme on the black board. He then suggested that the objectives must contain specific action verbs and should not be ambiguous. The participants were asked to revise their objectives so as to make them more specific. He then brought out the difference between learning and performance. While learning was an unseen process, performance could be seen, measured and repeated. In this light, he felt that the objectives must be able to satisfy a criterion test. For this, questions should be asked against each objective to see whether the objectives could answer the questions satisfactorily. A flow chart of the pre-production activities was then drawn on the board and each step in the chart was discussed in detail.

Each group was ask to write script on the topics already been selected by them.

**17th February, 1989 and 20th to 24th February, 1989**

*Group A:* ETV programme on the fuse wire and its use.

Team Members: Harsha Merchant, Sukhdeo Prakash Mathur, Vasudha Kamat.

On to 20th of February, 1989, the group finalised the script... consultations with the media experts. The talents needed for the film were finalised and the location for the video film was also chosen.

On the 21st, the final touches to the script were given after discussion with the producer, Mr. Balakrishnan and rehersals were carried out with the talents. In the afternoon, the film was shot.

On the 22nd, the continuity sheets were made prior to editing. The editing of the film commenced on the 23rd evening with the editor Mr. Vinod Kaul. It was contir ıed on the 24th and completed by the evening with the help of the editor and the producer Mr. Balakrishnan.

*Group B:* ETV Programme on 'Set Theory'

*Team Members:* Ravi Shankar Yadav, Kishor Desai and Pramod Chandra Sharma.

On the 20th of February the script was finalised after consultations with the media experts. On the 21st, discussions were held with Dr. M.C. Shamra and it was decided to get 15 students from the D.A.V. School for the shooting of the film. Students were briefed.

On the 2nd, the film was shot with the children. The shooting took up most part of the day.

On the 23rd, the rushes were seen by the participants and the cue sheets made. The film was edited on the 24th evening.

*Group C:* Tape Slide Programme on 'Geometrical shapes.

*Team Members:* Maharaj Kishen Kaul, Charan Pal Singh and Suman Yadav

On the 21st morning, after the script was finalised Prof. Bawa and Mr. Chainani were consulted at the I.P. Estate. On the 22nd morning, Mr. Chainani started framing the visuals according to the script. Paper cuttings were made throughout the day for the visuals.

On the 23rd, captions were made which were given for computer processing. The team members worked with Mr. Chainani for the art work and with Mr. O.P. Gupta for the 'Computer' processing. The templates were readied by the evening and the photography completed.

The finishing touches to the commentary were given on the 24th after the language of the commentary was checked by Dr. M.C. Sharma. The audio recording for background music was done at Mother School.

*Group D:* ETV film on Water Pollution

Team Members: Anil Bharatiya, Kitty Nanaya, Lakshmi Rao, Nirupma Jaimini.

On the 17th of February, 1989, the script was discussed

with Dr. Jagdish Singh, Dr. M.C. Sharma and Dr. Misra. Some suggested revisions were... then carried out. The team then previewed some films to get the required stock shots.

On the 20th of February, the script was finalised and the stock shots were selected.

On the 23rd, some shots required for the film were taken by Mr. Prem Lal the Cameramen. The same day, the audio-recording was done with the help of Sh. Vinod Kaul. In the evening the film was edited with the help of Mr. Yeshwant Rawat and the producer Mr. Balakrishnan.

On the 24th of February, the titles of the film and the music were added with the help of Sh. Vinod Kaul.

## MODULE VI

### Project Work

The last ten days of the course were taken up for project work. The participants were divided into four groups. Each group finalised one topic in consultation with. Resource Persons. Finally four topics i.e. one for tapeslide and three for ETV production were considered selected. The topic assigned for production to each group were:

*Group A:* ETV Programme on "The fuse wire and its use"

*Group B:* ETV Programme on "Set Theory"

*Group C:* Tapeslide Programme on "Geometrical Shapes"

*Group D:* ETV Programme on "Water Pollution."

The scripts along with objectives for the above programmes were finalised in consultation with experts from CIET. After that, production of the programmes was undertaken with the help of producer and technical staff of CIET. Different formats like demonstration drama and documentary, were used in the preparation of scripts for the programmes.

For the project on tape slide production, group—C was sent to GPE Division Indraprastha Wing of CIET where art work and slide were prepared. The audio recording was done at ER Divisions Mother School Wing of the Institute. Finally four programmes—one tapeslide and three ETV were prepared by the participants.

## EVALUATION & SUMMING UP SESSION

### Evaluation

On the concluding day, the success of the course was evaluated with the help of well designed strength weakness Action Programme (SWAP) PROFORMA". Most of the participants registered satisfaction of the course. Since the course was organised during shifting of studios, hardship in conducting practical work were felt. However, the suggestions of participants were recorded. Some of them were of view that intensive course in ETV production needed to be organised. Their suggestions of time management for devoting 3/4th of time for process of production like editing, shorting and handling of equipments were also noted. Observations of participants for inadequate facilities of technical staff, non-availability of suitable cameras and editing table were also noticed from SWAP proforma. They also desired more time for handling and operation of hardware. They expressed their feeling of adequate orientation of theoretical and practical dimension of E.T. in the course.

### Summing Up Session

The valedictory function of the course started with welcome of Chief Guest Prof. A.K. Sharma, Head, Department of Teacher Education, NCERT by Prof. C.H.K. Misra, the Course Director. Prof. Misra, pointed out the main objective of the course and expressed that this type of course had been organised by CIET for the first time. The experiences of this course would be useful for organising further courses.

Dr. M.C. Sharma, the course coordinator presented summary report of the course (Appendix). He pointed out that intensive efforts were made to achieve the objectives of the course, but due to limited resources for production, the programme produced by the participants are not of professional quality. Expressing his satisfaction for achieving the main objective of the course i.e. orientation towards theoretical and practical dimension of E.I., Dr. Sharma added that professional quality production need intensive training in production only which was not the objective of the course. He also expressed expectation from participants that they will utilise this training on the preparation of software needed for production. He desired that participants would not only involve themselves in training others but would also produce programme themselves and would be constantly interacting with CIET.

Preview of four programme was arranged and two participants also expressed their reaction about the course. According to them, the course had provided rich experiences. They also desired more time for production and "handling of equipments.

Prof. A.K. Sharma, the Chief Guest, distributed the certificates to participants' and wished them to utilise the rich experiences of the course in their respective institutions. He desired for qualitative software from teacher educators. According to him, software must be linked, with curriculum. He expressed that effective use of media must be based upon qualitative software production. He further expressed the need of educational programmes (ETV/audio/tapeslide) for training specially for new coming up institutions like DIET. He congratulated CIET for organising this type of course.

Prof. M.M. Chaudhri, Joint Director, CIET, in his presidential address said that one should be actually involved in production rather than getting training and training others. He stressed that special care must be taken for the management aspect of production. Emphasising the importance of enrichment programmes, Prof. Chaudhri pointed out that our ETV programme must be designed in such a way so that these could broaden the spectuary education. For this, one could even drift from the curriculum. Summarising the experiences for setting up SIET's he suggested that the utilisation of equipments (hardware) is more important rather than, only acquiring them. According to him, man power is insufficient in the field of ETV in our country. Dr. Chaudhari expected that teacher educators would try to handle and use the equipment. He further desired that participants of this course would try to involve themselves in actual production.

Dr. M.C. Sharma proposed a vote of thanks for the Chief Guest, the President, faculty, participants and their organisations. He expressed gratitude for the technical and secretarial staff for their active cooperation in organisation of the course.

# *APPENDIX - II*

## COURSE CONTENT

This course deals with basics of Educational Technology. It consists of six modules. Each module deals with one major aspect of E.T.

## MODULE I

### Theoretical Framework of Educational Technology

The module familiarises the participants with the concept and theoretical basis of E.T.

*Course content.* E.T.—meaning, nature and scope; Communication—process, principle of communication and relevance to educational media a modern learning theories/ instructional models and their applications in designing of instructions:

Systems approach—concept and its application in E.T., approaches in E.T.,—need, methods/techniques and utility in improving systems, programmes and materials.

Practical work—designing of instructions/Application of systems designing in ET. programme, audience profile need assessment and testing of scripts.

*Duration.* Six sessions each of one hour and practicum/ demonstration of 6 hours (total 12 hours).

*Mode of Interaction.* Lectures, Experimental Sessions, demonstrations, discussions.

## MODULE II

### Graphics

The module acquaints the participants with various aspects of graphic aids—their nature and potentialities.

*Course content.* Graphics aids in education—nature, types,

characteristics: Non-projected aids—charts, maps, globes, models, boards (type and process of production and utilisation), Projected aids—film strips, overhead transparencies, tapeslides.

*Practical work.* Operation and use of Hardware used in projected aids, Demonstration of Low Cost Teaching Aids and tapeslide programmes.

*Duration.* Time allotted to this module is 5 lectures each of 45-50 minutes duration and 5 hours for practical work.

*Mode of Interaction.* Lecture, demonstration, discussions, and practicum.

## MODULE III

### Audio/Radio Programmes

In this module, the participants would be acquainted with planning of content, development of script and production approaches/techniques in Radio/audio programmes.

*Course Content.* Audio/radio in education—planning of content and production approaches for formal and non-formal education, process of development of audio/radio programmes—scripting, format and production techniques evaluation—creative observation, formative and summative.

*Practical work.* Operation and use of Hardware of audio programmes, stages of programme production and evaluation of programmes.

*Duration.* 5 lectures each of 45-50 minutes duration and 4 hours for practicum are alloted for this module.

*Mode of Interaction.* Lectures, demonstrations, auditive practicum.

## MODULE IV

### ETV Programme

This module familiarises the participants with nature,

scope of ETV and acquaint with process of development and production of ETV programmes.

*Course Content.* Television in education—nature and scope; ETV curriculum—need and preparation; process of programme production—feed forward research, development of concept, production and evaluation; script writing for educational television—techniques and formats.

*Practical work.* Operation and use of hardware for ETV, play back of ETV programmes.

*Duration.* Time for this module is spread over 6 lectures (each of 45-50 minutes) and 6 hours for practicum.

*Model of Interaction.* Lecture, demonstration, preview, practicum.

## MODULE V

This module familiarise the participants with modes/ methods and importance of information and dissemination systems.

*Course content,* information and dissemination—needs,, methods and modes, media Resource Centre—Establishment and function, visit to Central Film Library.

*Duration.* 2 lectures of 45 minutes each.

*Mode of Interaction.* Lectures.

## MODULE VI

**Individual/Group Project**

In this, the participants would be required to specialise in production of material using one of the media such as graphics, projected aids, audio or video using principles of educational technology. This also includes evaluation of course.

*Duration.* 10 working days.

*Mode of Interaction.* Attachment Project method.

## LIST OF HANDOUTS

1. Educational Technology: A Modern Approach
2. System Approach
3. Modern Instructional Models and their application in designing instructions
4. Research in Educational Technology
5. Testing of ETV Programmes—Practicum
6. Graphics in Education
7. Visual Communication
8. Tape-slide Material in Education
9. Black Board
10. Low Cost Teaching Aids
11. Planning of Content and Production Approaches for Formal & Non-Formal Education
12. Process of Production and Techniques of Audio Programmes
13. Scripting Audio Programmes & Formats
14. Educational Television in India
15. Script Writing for TV
16. Scripting for Educational TV—Principles & Formats
17. Educational Communication by Television
18. ETV Curriculum for Teachers
19. The process of Television Production
20. ETV Transmission
21. Information & Dissemination

## ORIENTATION COURSE OF EDUCATIONAL TECHNOLOGY FOR TEACHERS EDUCATION

### Day-To-Day Programme

| | *Morning Session* | | | | *Afternoon Session* | |
|---|---|---|---|---|---|---|
| *Date* | *10.00—10.30 a.m. a.m.* | *10.30-11.30 a m. a.m.* | *11.45—1.00 a m. p.m.* | *2.00—3.00 p.m. p.m.* | *3.15-4.00 p m. p.m.* | *4.00—5.30 p.m. p.m.* |
| 31.1.89 | Registration | — Welcom/Introduction of participants<br>— Objectives of Course (MCS)<br>— Key note a—dress (JSR) | — Modern Approaches to E.T. (CHK) | Systems approach and its application in E.T. | Communication principle and process (CB) | Revelance of Communication to educational media. (CB) |
| 1.2.89 | Summary Report Presentation | Instructional Models & their application in designing instructions (MCS) | Practicum Application of systems designing/in ET Programme/Designing of Instructions. (SPM/MCS) | Research in ET-Method, Techniques. (JS) | Practicum/Demonstration related to Audience profile, need assessment, Testing of Script. (HMK) | |

*contd...*

| Date | Morning Session<br>10.00—10.30 a.m. a.m. | 10.30-11.30 a m. a.m. | 11.45—1.00 a m. p.m. | 2.00—3.00 p.m. p.m. | Afternoon Session<br>3.15-4.00 p m. p.m. | 4.00—5.30 p.m. p.m. |
|---|---|---|---|---|---|---|
| 2.2.89 | Summary Report | Graphics Aids in Education I (TRB) | Visual Communication (Demonstration of of Non-Project Aids (KKC) | | Non-projected Aids Boards-Types Characteristics. (SPM) | Low cost Teaching Aids HC/MCS |
| 3.2.89 | Presentation | Graphics Aids Charts (Process Production eradication) (TRB) | Projected Aids Films Stripts/OHT/Tape-slides. (KKC) | | Hardware used in Projected Aids. (MCS and | Screening of Tape-slide Pro- Technical Staff |
| 6.2.89 (Mon) | Summary | ETV in India (MMC) | ETV Curriculum need & preparation (CHK) | | Educational Communication by TV (CB) | Practicum Demonstration |
| 7.2.89 | Report | Scriptwriting for ETV—1 (GDS) | Techniques & Formats (Demonstration) (SPB) | | Scriptwriting —II (MP/GDS) | Short Exercises for Script writing (MP/MM/GDS) |
| 8.2.89 (Wed) | Presentation | Process of ETV Production-II Concept to programme (CB) | Operation and use of Hardware in ETV (AST) | | Process of ETV Production-II (CB) | ETV Production play back exercise |

| | | | | | |
|---|---|---|---|---|---|
| 9.2.89 | | Evaluation of ETV Programmes (JS) | ETV Transmission/play back of ETV Programmes (HL) | | Demonstration of ETV Studios facilities (AST) |
| 10.2.89 (Fri) | Information and Dissemination (SCV/SKC) | (. . . . . . . . . . . . . Educational Tour to IIMC/CCRT/DD. . . . . .) | | | |
| 13.2.89 (Mon) | Guidelines for Teachers ETV Programmes (JSR/SPB) | Preview of Teachers Programmes | Group work for Selection of Tonic/ Identification of Objectives etc. | | |

| | *Morning Session* | | *Afternoon Session* | |
|---|---|---|---|---|
| *Date* | *10.30—11.30* | *11.45—1.00* | *2.00—3.00* | *3.15—5.30* |
| 14.2.89 (Tue) | Audio/Radio in Education (LGS) | Planning of Content and production approaches for formal and Non-Formal Education (LGS) | Scripting of Radio/audio and formats (SP) | Process of production and techniques (SG) |
| 15.2.89 (Wed) at CIET, MSW | Evaluation in Audio/Radio (LGS) | Playback of Radio/Audio Programmes | Playback of Radio/Audio Programmes | Demonstration of Audio Studio/Recording etc. |
| 16.2.89 (Thurs) | Selection of Project | Group formation | Analysis, reference work, | briefs etc. |
| 17th & 20th to Feb. 89 | Project work for | (A) Tape Slide programme Production (TRB GEP STAFF) | (B) Audio/Radio Programme (LGS & STAFF) | Production (C) ETV prog. production (CB & ETV STAFF) |
| 27.2.89 (Mon.) | Evaluation of Course/Valedictory | | TA/DA Disbursement | |

## SUMMARY REPORT OF THE COURSE

***—Dr. M.C. Sharma,***
*Course Coordinator*

The course was intended to orient teacher educators towards theoretical and practical dimensions of Educational Technology so that they could in turn train teachers in their respective Institutions.

The specific objectives of the course were:

— to familiarise participants with theoretical basis of educational Technology.

— to orient them towards characteristics and potential of different types of Graphics aids and Media (small format and Mass).

— to acquaint them with process of development of different types of Graphics aids, Audi's/Radio & ETV Programmes.

— to familiarise them with Hardware (equipment) used in the production of tape slide/Radio-audio, ETV programmes.

— to impart practical experiences in preparation of instructional materials/scripts used for different types of Graphic aids/media.

— to make, them aware about the utilisation, evaluation & dissemination of various types of broadcasting & non-broadcasting programmes.

On the basis of the objectives, the course was divided into six modules.

| | | |
|---|---|---|
| *Modules I* | — | Theoretical framework of Educational Technology. |
| *Module II* | — | Graphics. |
| *Module II* | — | Audio/Radio programmes. |

*Module IV* — ETV programmes.
*Module V* — Information and dissemination.
*Module VI* — Project work for production of Tape-slide, audio or video programmes using principles

The first two days of the course devoted to discussing the theoretical basis of Educational Technology like concept, the application of systems approach, Instructional models and evaluation. Practicum exercises were also conducted in this model. In the next two days, the graphic aids in education— their process and production — were discussed in details,

In the second week of the course, the module and programmes was taken up. This included sessions on ETV in India, ETV animation, script writing for ETV, process of production and evaluation of programmes. The participants were also given practicum exercises on script writing in the same week the module on information and dissemination was also completed. The participants previewed many films during the sessions for evaluation. Educational tour to Central Production Centre, Doordarshan was also arranged where participants were shown the largest Computerised equipments and lighting systems used in studios.

In the third week, the module on Audio/Radio was taken up. Various formats for writing scripts for audio programmes were discussed and a number of Audio/Radio programmes were played back for the participants. In the two sessions on ETV and Audio/Radio, the participants were shown the various hardware used in ETV and Audio/Radio.

The last ten days of the course were taken up for project work. The participants were divided into four groups and the following projects were finalised:

*Group A* — ETV Programme on "The fuse wire".
*Group B* — ETV Programme on "Set theory".

*Group C* — ETV Programme on "Water Pollution."

*Group D* — Tape-Slide Programme on "Geometrical Shapes".

The scripts for the above programmes were finalised in consultation with the experts at CIET. This was followed by the production of the programmes with the help of the producer and the technical staff of CIET. It may be mentioned here that different formats like demonstration, drama and documentary were used in the scripts. The script of the tape-slide programme was finalised and the group was sent to I.P. Estate for art work and preparation of slides. The audio recording was done at the Mother School Wing of the CIET. On the last day, the course was evaluated by the participants and their suggestions received.

Although great efforts were taken to achieve the objectives of the course, due to limitations of the resources available for production, the programmes produced by the participants are not of professional quality. But the main objective of the course was to Orient the participants towards the process of production and not make them professional producers. And it was in this context that the productions were done.

It is hoped that the participants who are teacher educators have been benefited by the course as far as preparation of software is concerned and they would have been enlightened with the process of production of different aids and media needed for Educational Programmes. We also have expectations from participants of the course that they besides training teachers in their institutions will also involve themselves in preparation of softwares and production of educational programmes for small format and mass media. They will also remain in touch with us by informing us about their creative work in the field of Educational Technology.

## VIDEO EQUIPMENT REQUIRED FOR EDUCATIONAL TECHNOLOGY

| S.No. | Equipment | Qty. | Cost (approx.) | Source of supply |
|---|---|---|---|---|
| | **VCR** | (J. Yen) | 100 | Y=12 Rs. |
| 1. | EV-A 300E | 1 | 1,09,000 | Sony Video System Sony Corporation Tokyo, Japan |
| 2. | EV—S 700E | 1 | 2,10,000 | |
| | **Camera with Recorder** | | | |
| 3. | CCD-V8 AF-EK | 2 pcs | 5,14,000 | " |
| | **Remote Editing Control** | | | |
| 4. | Vido Editing Controller RM-E 100 | 1 pcs | 25,800 | " |
| | **Monitors—Audio/Video** | | | |
| 5. | PVM—6030 ME Trinitron Color | 2 pc | 1,70,600 | " |
| | OR | | | |
| | PVM—1371 OM Trinitron Color | 2 pcs | 3,08,000 | " |
| | **AC Power Adapter** | | | |
| 6. | AC—V&E | 1 pc | 28,900 | " |
| | **Batteries** | | | |
| 7. | NP—22 Rechargable Batteries | 20 pcs | 80,000 | " |
| | **Tripod** | | | |
| 8. | VCT—600 | 2 pcs | 71,800 | " |
| | **Video Cassette Winder/ Eraser** | | | |
| 9. | BE—V 8 | 1 pc | 17,400 | " |
| 10. | Battery Charger BC—1 WA | 1 pc | 62,100 | " |
| 11. | LC—V 605 Carrying case | 2 pcs | 43,000 | |
| 12. | LC— V&5 Video Camera Jacket | 2 pcs | 13,000 | " |

| S.No. | Equipment | Qty. | Cost (approx.) | Source of supply |
|---|---|---|---|---|
| 13. | Cables | | 1,00,000 | |
| | (i) EURO Connector Cable (for Audio/ Video) | | | |
| | (ii) Other reqd. cables-to make the system complete from Sony. | | | SONY Video System Sony Corporation Tokyo, Japan |
| 14. | Non Recorded Video Cassettes (Tape) | | | |
| | (1) P 5—30 | 10 | 15,000 | " |
| | (2) P 5—60 | 10 | 17,000 | " |
| | (3) P 5—90 | 10 | 23,000 | " |
| 15. | VHS VCR | 1 | 15,000 | Local Market |
| 16. | Colour TV Set | 2 | 20,000 | " |
| 17. | Console for setting up of the system | 2 nets | 12,000 | " |
| 18. | Power Cable, Video and Audio Cable | — | 5,000 | " |

# Select Bibliography


Ausubel, D. 'In Defence of advance organisers : A reply to the Critics', Review of Educational Research, 1978,48, pp. 251-257.

Barnes, B.R. and Clawson, E.V. 'Do advance Organisers facilitate learning? Recommendations for further research based on an analysis of thirty-two studies'. Review of Educational Research, 1975, 45,637-659.

Bell, J.E.: *Projective Technique* (Longmans, Green and Co., NY. 1948).

Bloom, Benjaim S. *Stability and Change in Human Characteristics,* New York: Wiley, 1964.

Bossing, N.L., *Teaching in Secondary School,* 3rd ed. Boston: Houghton Mifflin Co.. 1952. Chapters II, 12, 13.

Brunner, J., Goodnow, J.J. and Austin GA. 'A Study of Thinking' New York, John Wiley, 1977.

Buros, D.K. (ed): *The Fifth Mental Measurements Year Book.* (Highland Park, NY. 1959).

Cantor, N., *The Teaching-Learning Process.* New York: The Dryden Press, Inc., 1953. Chapter 3.

Chauhan, S.S., *Advance Educational Psychology* (Vikas, New Delhi, 1978).

Coombs, Philip H., *The World Educational Crisis,* New York: Oxford University Press, 1968.

Council of Europe, *Permanent Education, A Compendium of Studies,* Strasbourg: Council of Europe, 1970.

Cronback, Lee. J., *Essential of Psychological Testing* (Harper and Brothers, NY. 1960).

Dave, R.H., *Towards a Theory of Educational Extension, Teacher*

*Education* 10, No. 4 (1986), New Delhi: National Council of Educational Research and Training.

Douglas, H.R., and H. H. Mills, *Teaching in High School* New York: The Ronald Press Co., 1948. Chapter 11.

Freeman, F.S., *Theory and Practice of Psychological Testing.* (Holt Richart, NY. 1962).

Garrison, N.L., *Improvement of Teaching.* New York: The Dryden Press, Inc., 1955. Chapter 5.

Grambs, J.D., and W. Iverson, *Modern Methods in Secondary Education.* New York: William Sloane Associates. 1952. Chapter 4.

Greenough, Richard, *Adult Education and National Development. UNESCO Chronicle* 18, No. 4 (1972), pp. 131-134.

Guthrie, E.R., *The Psychology of Learning,* rev. ed. New York: Harper and Brothers, Publishers, 1952. Chapter 12.

Hansen, K.H., *High School Teaching.* New Jersey: Prentice Hall, Inc., 1957. Chapter 7.

Hartely, J. and Davies, I.K., "Preinstructional Strategies: The role of pre-tests-behavioural objectives, overviews, and advance organisers". Review of Educational Research, 1976, 46, pp. 239-265.

Hershfield, A.F., *Minorities,' United States of America* in *Distance Education: A Spectrum of Case Studies (1990),* (Eds. Koul, B.N. and Jenkins, J.), Kogan Page. London.

Hilgard, E.R., *Theories of Learning.* New York: Appleton-Century Crofts, Inc.. 1948.

Houle, C.O., "Continued Professional Education in the USA, *Lifelong Learning—A Symposium on Continuing Education* edited by F.W. Jessup. Oxford., Pergamon, 1969.

Illich, Ivan, *Deschooling Society, World Perspectives.* New York: Harper and Row, 1970.

Jessup, F.W., ed., *Lifelong Learning—A Symposium on Continuing Education.* Oxford: Pergamon, 1969.

Johnson, E., and R.E. Michael, *Principles of Teaching.* Boston: Allyn and Bacon, Inc., 1958. Chapter 6.

Joyce, B.R. and Weil, M., 'Models of Teaching' (2nd Ed.), Printice Hall, 1980.

Kingsiey, H.L., *The Nature and Conditions of Learning.* New York: Prentice-Hall, Inc., 1946. Chapter 6.

Klausmeier, H.J., 'Educational Experience and Cognitive Development', Educational Psychologist, 1977, 12, pp. 179-196, Quoted by Encyclopaedia of Educational Research. Fifth Edition, Vol. 2,1982, pp. 891-916.

Klausmeier, H.J., and Feldman, K.V. 'Effect of a definition and a Varying number of examples and non-examples on concept attainment'. Journal of educational Psychology, 1975, 67, pp. 174-178.

Klausmeier, H.T., and Harris C.W. Analysis of Concept Learning, Academic Press, New York, London, 1966, pp. 1-17.

Koul, B.N., *Need for Professional Training in Distance Education* (1984), (Ed. Parmaji. S.), Sterling Publishers Pvt. Ltd., New Delhi.

Lawton, J.T. and Wanska, S.K., 'Advance Organiser as a teaching strategy. A reply to Barnes and Clawson.' Review of Educational Research, 1977,47, pp. 233-244.

Laxshmi. Verbal Concept Learning-A Study, Chugh Publication, Allahabad. 1976.

Le Veugle, Jean, *Initigtion a l'education permanente.* Paris: UNESCO, 1970.

Lengrand, Paul, L'Education des adultes et le concept del' education permanente." Convergence 3, No. 2 (1970).

Leona, E. Tyler, *Tests and Measurements* (Prentice Hall, NY. 1973).

Lister, I., "The Concept of Deschooling and the Future of Secondary Education, Mimeographed. Amsterdam: European Cultural Foundation, 1971.

Maneu, Rene, "Pour une education permanente," *Convergence* 1, No. 1 (1968).

Mayer, R.E., 'Advance Organisers that compensate for the

organisation of text,' Journal of Educational Psychology, 1978, 70, pp. 880-886.

Mayer, R.E., 'Can advance organisers influence meaningful learning?' Review of Educational Research, 1979, 49, pp. 371-383.

Mead, Margaret, *Culture and Commitment: A Study of the Generation Gap.* Garden City, N.J.: Natural History Press, 1970.

Melvin, A.G., *General Methods of Teaching.* New York: McGraw-Hill Book Company, Inc., 1952. Chapter 5.

Morrison, H.C., *The Practice of Teaching in the Secondary School.* Chicago: University of Chicago Press, 1931 (revised). Chapters 14-17.

Mortensen, Dpmaid G., *Guidance in Today's Schools* (John Wiley and Sons, New York, 1972).

Myers, George E., *Principles and Techniques of Guidance,* (McGraw Hill Book Co., New York, 1976).

Schramm, W. et. al., *The New Media Memo to Educational Planners.* Paris: UNESCO International Institute for Educational Planning, 1967.

Shertzsr Stone, *Fundamentals of Guidance* (Houghton Miftlin Co., Boston, 1976).

Skinner, C.E. and others, *Educational Psychology.* New Jersey: Prentice-Hall, Inc., 1955. Chapter 17.

Smith, H.P., "Individual Differences in Ability to Learn," in *Psychology in Teaching.* New Jersey: Prentice-Hall, Inc., 1954. Chapter 10.

Stephens, J.M., *Educational Psychology.* New York: Henry Holt and Company, 1951. Chapter 3.

Voeks, V.W., "Formalisation and Clarification of a Theory of Learning," *Journal of Psychology,* 1950. pp. 30, 341-362.

# Index

❑❑❑